# Experimenting with Everyday Science

# Man-Made Materials

Stephen M. Tomecek

CHELSEA HOUSE
PUBLISHERS
An imprint of Infobase Publishing

*In memory of my father, John S. Tomecek, who taught me how to appreciate the natural world and man's many additions to it. Thank you for always being there for me.*

**Experimenting with Everyday Science: Man-Made Materials**

Copyright © 2011 by Infobase Publishing

Chelsea House
An imprint of Infobase Publishing
132 West 31st Street
New York, NY 10001

**Library of Congress Cataloging-in-Publication Data**
Tomecek, Steve.
  Man-made materials / Stephen M. Tomecek.
    p. cm. — (Experimenting with everyday science)
  Includes bibliographical references and index.
  ISBN 978-1-60413-175-8 (hardcover)
  1. Synthetic products—Juvenile literature. I. Title. II. Title: Manmade materials. III. Series.
  TA403.2.T66 2010
  620.1'1078—dc22     2010009981

Chelsea House books are available at special discounts when purchased in bulk quantities for businesses, associations, institutions, or sales promotions. Please call our Special Sales Department in New York at (212) 967-8800 or (800) 322-8755.

You can find Chelsea House on the World Wide Web at http://www.chelseahouse.com.

Text design by Annie O'Donnell
Cover design by Alicia Post
Composition by Mary Susan Ryan-Flynn
Illustrations by Sholto Ainslie for Infobase Publishing
Cover printed by Bang Printing, Brainerd, Minn.
Book printed and bound by Bang Printing, Brainerd, Minn.
Date printed: November 2010
Printed in the United States of America

10 9 8 7 6 5 4 3 2 1

This book is printed on acid-free paper.

All links and Web addresses were checked and verified to be correct at the time of publication. Because of the dynamic nature of the Web, some addresses and links may have changed since publication and may no longer be valid.

# Contents

# Introduction

When you hear the word *science*, what's the first thing that comes to mind? If you are like most people, it's probably an image of a laboratory filled with tons of glassware and lots of sophisticated equipment. The person doing the science is almost always wearing a white lab coat and probably is looking rather serious while engaged in some type of experiment. While there are many places where this traditional view of a scientist still holds true, labs aren't the only place where science is at work. Science can also be found at a construction site, on a basketball court, and at a concert by your favorite band. The truth of the matter is that science is happening all around us. It's at work in the kitchen when we cook a meal, and we can even use it when we paint a picture. Architects use science when they design a building, and science also explains why your favorite baseball player can hit a home run.

In **Experimenting with Everyday Science**, we are going to examine some of the science that we use in our day-to-day lives. Instead of just talking about the science, these books are designed to put the science right in your hands. Each book contains about 25 experiments centering on one specific theme. Most of the materials used in the experiments are things that you can commonly find around your house or school. Once you are finished experimenting, it is our hope that you will have a better understanding of how the world around you works. While reading these books may not make you a world-class athlete or the next top chef, we hope that they inspire you to discover more about the science behind everyday things and encourage you to make the world a better place!

# Safety Precautions

## REVIEW BEFORE STARTING ANY EXPERIMENT

Each experiment includes special safety precautions that are relevant to that particular project. These do not include all the basic safety precautions that are necessary whenever you are working on a scientific experiment. For this reason, it is necessary that you read and remain mindful of the General Safety Precautions that follow.

Experimental science can be dangerous, and good laboratory procedure always includes carefully following basic safety rules. Things can happen very quickly while you are performing an experiment. Materials can spill, break, or even catch fire. There will be no time after the fact to protect yourself. Always prepare for unexpected dangers by following the basic safety guidelines during the entire experiment, whether or not something seems dangerous to you at a given moment.

We have been quite sparing in prescribing safety precautions for the individual experiments. For one reason, we want you to take very seriously every safety precaution that is printed in this book. If you see it written here, you can be sure that it is here because it is absolutely critical.

Read the safety precautions here and at the beginning of each experiment before performing each activity. It is difficult to remember a long set of general rules. By rereading these general precautions every time you set up an experiment, you will be reminding yourself that lab safety is critically important. In addition, use your good judgment and pay close attention when performing potentially dangerous procedures. Just because the text does not say "be careful with hot liquids" or "don't cut yourself with a knife" does not mean that you can be careless when boiling water or punching holes in plastic bottles. Notes in the text are special precautions to which you must pay special attention.

## GENERAL SAFETY PRECAUTIONS

Accidents caused by carelessness, haste, insufficient knowledge, or taking an unnecessary risk can be avoided by practicing safety procedures and being alert while conducting experiments. Be sure to check the individual experiments in this book for additional safety regulations and adult supervision requirements. If you will be working in a lab, do not work alone. When you are working off site, keep in groups with a minimum of three students per group, and follow school rules and state legal requirements for the number of supervisors required. Ask an adult supervisor with basic training in first aid to carry a small first-aid kit. Make sure everyone knows where this person will be during the experiment.

## PREPARING

- Clear all surfaces before beginning experiments.
- Read the instructions before you start.
- Know the hazards of the experiments and anticipate dangers.

## PROTECTING YOURSELF

- Follow the directions step-by-step.
- Do only one experiment at a time.
- Locate exits, fire blanket and extinguisher, master gas and electricity shut-offs, eyewash, and first-aid kit.
- Make sure there is adequate ventilation.
- Do not horseplay.
- Keep floor and workspace neat, clean, and dry.
- Clean up spills immediately.
- If glassware breaks, do not clean it up; ask for teacher assistance.
- Tie back long hair.
- Never eat, drink, or smoke in the laboratory or workspace.
- Do not eat or drink any substances tested unless expressly permitted to do so by a knowledgeable adult.

## USING EQUIPMENT WITH CARE

- Set up apparatus far from the edge of the desk.
- Use knives or other sharp-pointed instruments with care.
- Pull plugs, not cords, when removing electrical plugs.
- Clean glassware before and after use.
- Check glassware for scratches, cracks, and sharp edges.
- Clean up broken glassware immediately.
- Do not use reflected sunlight to illuminate your microscope.
- Do not touch metal conductors.
- Use alcohol-filled thermometers, not mercury-filled thermometers.

## USING CHEMICALS

- Never taste or inhale chemicals.
- Label all bottles and apparatus containing chemicals.
- Read labels carefully.
- Avoid chemical contact with skin and eyes (wear safety glasses, lab apron, and gloves).
- Do not touch chemical solutions.
- Wash hands before and after using solutions.
- Wipe up spills thoroughly.

## HEATING SUBSTANCES

- Wear safety glasses, apron, and gloves when boiling water.
- Keep your face away from test tubes and beakers.
- Use test tubes, beakers, and other glassware made of Pyrex glass.
- Never leave apparatus unattended.
- Use safety tongs and heat-resistant gloves.

- If your laboratory does not have heat-proof workbenches, put your Bunsen burner on a heat-proof mat before lighting it.
- Take care when lighting your Bunsen burner; light it with the airhole closed, and use a Bunsen burner lighter in preference to wooden matches.
- Turn off hot plates, Bunsen burners, and gas when you are done.
- Keep flammable substances away from flames and other sources of heat.
- Have a fire extinguisher on hand.

## FINISHING UP

- Thoroughly clean your work area and any glassware used.
- Wash your hands.
- Be careful not to return chemicals or contaminated reagents to the wrong containers.
- Do not dispose of materials in the sink unless instructed to do so.
- Clean up all residues and put them in proper containers for disposal.
- Dispose of all chemicals according to all local, state, and federal laws.

## BE SAFETY CONSCIOUS AT ALL TIMES!

# Building a
# Better World

We live in a manufactured world. Everywhere you turn, you find objects made by humans to help us get through our day-to-day lives: Among them are roads and the vehicles that we drive on them, buildings, and sidewalks. Inside our homes, we have appliances, furniture, clothing, and devices that keep us entertained. Even much of the food we eat and the medicines we take are produced or processed in factories.

Today, almost everything that we use has some type of man-made material in it, on it, or around it. Most people never think about it, but these modern materials have some serious science behind them. Each time you brush your teeth, comb your hair, and wash your face, you are using materials that scientists helped to create. Most of the clothes that we wear have some **synthetic fibers** in them, and so do the products we use to construct our homes and schools. These days, materials science is big business, and its effect on our lives continues to grow.

The development of man-made materials did not happen overnight. It has been a slow, steady progression that has taken thousands of years. Early in human history, manufactured products were made using natural materials that came directly from the surrounding environment. Rocks were used for tools. Trees and other plants were used to make shelters. Animal hides were used for clothing. As time progressed, people discovered that they could change the properties of natural materials, creating new materials. As a result of the human desire to create new and better materials, the science of chemistry was born.

Chemistry is the branch of science that looks at matter and how it changes. *Matter* is the term scientists use to describe all of the substances found in the universe. Matter comes in several different forms, or physical states: solid, liquid, gas, and plasma. Every type of matter—from the water we drink and the air we breathe to the rocks under our feet and the food we eat—is made from a small number of chemical "building blocks" called elements. To date, scientists have discovered 118 chemical elements, each with a unique set of properties. Like the letters in an alphabet, chemical elements can be combined. Yet, instead of creating words, they make substances called compounds.

Matter can change in two ways. A physical change alters the size, shape, or state of a substance, but the substance itself remains the same. An ice cube melting or a puddle evaporating is a physical change. In each case, the substance involved is still water. The only thing that has changed is its physical state. Another important feature of most physical changes is that they can be reversed. You can melt and freeze a container of water as many times as you want, simply by changing how hot or cold you make it.

This is not the case with a chemical change. When a chemical change occurs, the composition of a substance is altered and a new substance forms. A chemical change cannot be reversed. One simple chemical change is burning a piece of wood. Another would be cooking an egg. In both these examples, a change has occurred that has created a new substance. You cannot "un-burn" a piece of wood or "un-cook" the egg.

One of the earliest discoveries involving chemical changes concerned the effects of heat on earth materials. People made pots and bricks of mud and clay that were dried in the sun. Sun-dried bricks work fairly well in dry climates, but when they are exposed to water, they tend to fall apart. Over time, people discovered that when pots made from clay were placed in a fire, they became much harder and more resistant to wear. This was probably an accidental discovery, but soon people began intentionally "firing" other natural earth substances in an attempt to change their properties. In the process, they created a number of new building materials. One of these products was a white powder, known today as **plaster** of Paris. In **Experiment 1: *Building with Plaster of Paris***, you will experiment with plaster of Paris and discover how its unique properties can be put to use in several ways.

# Building with Plaster of Paris

## Topic

What properties of plaster of Paris make it a useful building material?

## Introduction

Building with plaster is one of the oldest known techniques. Some of the earliest types of plaster were made from natural substances such as clay, soil, and even animal dung. When one of these materials was mixed with water, it formed a thick paste that was spread over the outside of reed and wooden shelters. When the paste dried, it formed a hard shell, providing added protection from wind and rain. As people experimented with new materials, they discovered that a more durable and attractive plaster could be made from heating and crushing the mineral gypsum. Over the years, this material has become known as plaster of Paris, because one major production center in the 1700s was located near Paris, France. Today, plaster of Paris is used for a variety of jobs. In this activity, you will conduct several experiments to determine why plaster of Paris is such a popular material.

## Time Required

60 minutes

## Materials

- small box of plaster of Paris (available at most home improvement or art supply stores)
- large disposable plastic bowl
- water
- disposable plastic spoon
- 6-in. x 6-in. (15-cm x 15-cm) piece of window screen
- large disposable paper or plastic plate
- disposable plastic cup (6 oz, or 200 mL)

- rubber gloves

- dust mask

- goggles or safety glasses

- piece of sandpaper

- screwdriver

- hammer

- watch or clock

- roll of paper towels

- adult to assist you

---

**Safety Note** During this experiment, you will be working with plaster of Paris. The liquid plaster can cause irritation and a burning sensation if it gets on unprotected skin. You might want to wear a dust mask, rubber gloves, and safety glasses when mixing and pouring the plaster. If plaster gets on unprotected skin, wash immediately with soap and water. If any of the liquid plaster mixture spills, clean it up immediately with a wet paper towel. It is recommended that you conduct this activity under the supervision of a responsible adult.

---

## Procedure

1. Put on the safety glasses. Open the container of plaster and rub a small amount of dry plaster between your thumb and forefinger to feel the texture. Wash and dry your hands and then put on the gloves. Record your observations on the data table. Use the plastic cup to measure 2 cups (500 mL) of dry plaster into the bowl. Add 1 cup (250 mL) of cold water to the bowl. Use the spoon to stir the plaster and water until they are evenly mixed. Observe the texture of the mixture as you stir and record your observations on the data table.

2. Lay the piece of screen flat on the plate. Pour a small amount of plaster from the bowl onto the screen and use the back of the spoon to spread the plaster mixture evenly over the entire screen. Place the plate in a safe location and allow it to stand undisturbed for about 30 minutes.

3. Pour the remaining plaster mixture into the cup so that it is about ¾ full. Place the spoon into the middle of the cup so that the handle is sticking straight up. (See Figure 1.) Allow the cup to stand undisturbed for 30 to 40 minutes.

**Figure 1**

© Infobase Publishing

**4.** After 30 minutes have passed, pick up the piece of window screen that you coated with plaster. Slowly bend it and observe what happens. Note the texture of the plaster and record your observations on the data sheet. Rub the plaster gently with the sandpaper and observe what happens.

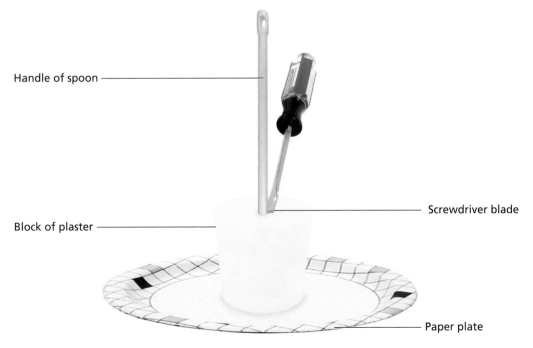

**Figure 2**

© Infobase Publishing

5. Check to see if the plaster in the cup has hardened. If it has, carefully peel away the plastic cup and place the plaster with the spoon in it on the plate. Place the blade of the screwdriver next to the handle of the spoon and use the hammer to tap it gently until you split the block of plaster in two (see Figure 2). Remove the spoon from the plaster and observe the inside of the plaster block. Record your observations on the data table.

| Data Table 1 | |
| --- | --- |
| **Sample** | **Observations** |
| Wet plaster mixture | |
| Texture of dry plaster on screen | |
| Reaction of dry plaster on screen to being bent | |
| Texture of dry plaster on screen after being rubbed with sandpaper | |
| Inside of plaster block with spoon after being split with the screwdriver | |

## Analysis

1. How did the dry plaster feel when it first came out of the container?
2. What was the texture of the plaster when you mixed it with the water?
3. What happened to the window screen after the plaster dried? What happened to the plaster when you rubbed it with the sandpaper?
4. How did the inside of the plaster block look after you split it and removed the spoon?

## What's Going On?

Plaster of Paris is made from gypsum, which is a common sedimentary rock formed when mineral-rich water evaporates. When gypsum is heated to about 250°F (120°C), it undergoes a chemical change and "dehydrates," losing as much as 75% of the water that was originally trapped in the crystals. When the dehydrated gypsum is crushed into a powder, it is called plaster of Paris. The chemical name of plaster of Paris is calcium sulfate hemihydrate.

Historians are not certain when people first began making plaster from gypsum, but there is evidence to suggest that it was used more than 9,000 years ago in what is now Syria. By 4500 B.C., Egyptian builders were using gypsum-based plaster as a **mortar** between stone blocks. They also used it to cover many monuments, including the Great Pyramid of Cheops. By Roman times, people were using plaster to make copies of statues and other works of art. During the Middle Ages, it was used to decorate the interior of churches and cathedrals.

In our modern world, plaster of Paris has many uses, including covering or patching holes in walls. Plaster can be sanded smooth, or it can be left with a rough texture to give the appearance of stucco. It can be painted any color or covered with wallpaper. Many sculptors use plaster of Paris because it can be easily carved when it is hard and can be poured into molds when it is liquid. One of the most important uses of plaster of Paris is in medicine. Doctors frequently use plaster casts to help protect and set broken bones.

## Our Findings

1. The dry plaster powder felt smooth and slippery.
2. The liquid plaster was a thick paste.
3. The window screen became stiff, and the plaster filled in all the holes. When the screen bent, the plaster began to crack. When the plaster was sanded, it became very smooth.
4. After the plaster block was split, the two pieces had an impression of the spoon.

## MAKING A DRY WALL

As you discovered in the previous experiment, one special property of plaster of Paris is that when it is a liquid, it can be easily spread over a surface and will quickly dry to produce a smooth, hard finish. During the last century, one of the most common techniques used for creating the interior walls of buildings was plaster and **lath** construction. This method involves building a wall frame using a number of evenly spaced vertical studs. Thin strips of wood, called lath, are nailed across the studs. The wall is then covered with a layer of plaster. The plaster seeps into the spaces between the lath strips, helping to hold it in place. When the first layer of plaster hardens, additional layers of plaster are added to produce a wall with a smooth, even surface.

Making a wall with plaster and lath can produce excellent results, but it also has a downside. First, it takes a lot of time and work. In addition, if the plaster is not applied properly, it can bow out, making a wall uneven. By the mid-twentieth century, most homebuilders had given up on using plaster and lath in favor of a new technique called **drywall** construction. As you will discover in **Experiment 2:** *Drywall vs. Plaster*, this man-made material offers many of the same benefits as plaster with far fewer problems.

# EXPERIMENT 2

# Drywall vs. Plaster

## Topic

How does drywall compare with plaster for wall construction?

## Introduction

For centuries, the traditional way of making interior building walls was to use plaster of Paris spread over wooden boards called lath, which were nailed to the frame of the wall. This "wet wall" construction technique was time consuming and expensive, because several coats of plaster were needed to cover each wall. Before a new coat was added, the previous layer had to be completely dry. In 1916, the U.S. Gypsum Company developed a new building material called drywall to replace plaster and lath construction. This product was a rigid plasterboard that was sandwiched between two pieces of heavy paper. Instead of having to build up a wall over time using wet plaster, drywall sheets could be nailed in place directly over the wall frame. At first, many builders would not use drywall because they felt that it was inferior to plaster. In this experiment, you will compare drywall to plaster to evaluate the performance of each material.

## Time Required

60 minutes

## Materials

- small box of plaster of Paris (available at most home improvement or art supply stores)
- large disposable plastic bowl
- 16 oz (500 mL) disposable plastic cup
- water
- wide-bladed putty knife or paint scraper

- 12-in. x 6-in. (30-cm x 15-cm) piece of window screen

- 12-in. x 6-in. (30-cm x 15-cm) piece of ½-in.-thick drywall (also called plasterboard or sheetrock; available at building supply or home improvement stores)

- 4 pieces of 2 x 4 wood, each 6-in.-long (15 cm)

- 8 wide-head nails, each 1-in.-long (2 cm)

- hammer

- ruler

- small container of water-based paint

- small paintbrush

- rubber gloves

- goggles or safety glasses

- watch or clock

- old newspapers to cover table

- paper towels

- adult to assist you

**Safety Note** During this experiment, you will be working with plaster of Paris. The liquid plaster can cause irritation and a burning sensation if it contacts skin. You may want to wear rubber gloves and safety glasses when mixing and spreading the liquefied plaster. If plaster gets on your skin, wash immediately with mild soap and water. If any of the liquid plaster mixture spills, clean it up immediately with a wet paper towel. It is recommended that you conduct this activity under the supervision of a responsible adult.

## Procedure

1. Spread several layers of old newspaper on the table to protect the surface. Put on the safety glasses. Place the bowl on the newspapers and use the plastic cup to measure 2 cups (500 mL) of dry plaster into the bowl. Add 1 cup (250 mL) of cold water to the bowl. Use the putty knife to stir the plaster and water until they are evenly mixed. If necessary, add more water, but do not make the plaster too runny. It should be the consistency of thick paste. Observe the texture of the mixture as you stir.

2. Take two of the wood blocks and place them on top of the newspapers so they are parallel to each other with a 9-in. (22-cm) space between them. Place the piece of screen across the blocks so that it forms a bridge. (See Figure 1.) Hammer one nail at each corner of the screen so that the screen is attached to the wood blocks. Using the putty knife, spread a small amount of the plaster mixture evenly over the entire screen. Keep adding plaster and spreading it until it covers the screen and is about ¼ in. (10 mm) thick. Try to make the surface of the plaster as smooth as possible. When you are finished, allow the screen to stand undisturbed for about 30 minutes.

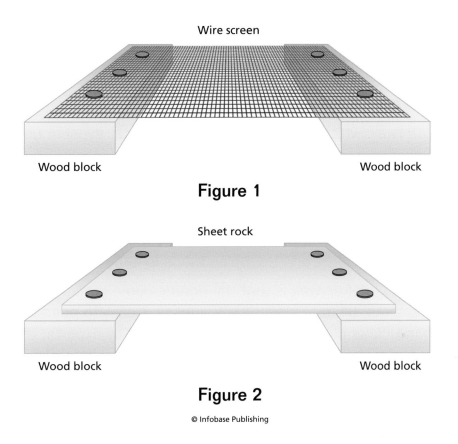

Wire screen

Wood block                    Wood block

**Figure 1**

Sheet rock

Wood block                    Wood block

**Figure 2**

© Infobase Publishing

3. Take the other two wood blocks and place them on the table as you did in Step 2. Lay the piece of drywall on top of the wood blocks so that the white side is facing up. Nail the drywall to the blocks as you did with the screen in Step 2. (See Figure 2.) Place the drywall bridge next to the screen.

4. After 30 minutes have passed, observe the two bridges. Run your hand over them and compare their textures. Place one hand on the middle of each "bridge" and gently press down. Observe what happens to the surface of each as you increase the pressure. Use the paint and brush to paint a small section of each bridge and compare the way they look as you apply the paint.

## Analysis

1. What problems, if any, did you encounter when you applied the plaster to the screen?

2. How did the texture of the dry plaster compare with the surface of the drywall?

3. How did the surface of the plaster and the drywall react when you applied pressure to each?

4. How did the surface of the drywall compare with the surface of the plaster as you painted each?

5. Based on your experiment, does drywall offer any advantages over plaster when it comes to making a wall?

### What's Going On?

Drywall, which is also known as **sheetrock**, gypsum board, and plasterboard, offers many advantages over plaster and lath when it comes to constructing a wall. First, it is much less time consuming to use. Because a wall constructed with plaster needs to dry between coats, it can take a week or more to complete. Using sheetrock, workers can put up the same wall in about two days. A sheetrock wall needs plaster only to fill the seams between the boards and the holes made by the screws or nails.

A second advantage of drywall is that the boards come prefinished. A drywall board has a smooth, uniform surface that makes it easy to paint or cover with wallpaper. Unless plaster and lath walls are built by experts, they often have uneven surfaces. This means they must be sanded before they can be painted.

One final advantage of using drywall boards is that they come in standard sizes that can be easily trimmed to fit almost any space. They are perfect for "do it yourselfers." These days, drywall has replaced plaster and lath in most new construction, although plaster is still often used for historical structures that are being remodeled using traditional building methods.

### Our Findings

1. It is difficult to evenly spread the wet plaster over a surface.

2. The drywall is much smoother and uniform in thickness.

3. They both bent. The drywall flexed, but as the plaster bent, it began to crack on the surface.

4. The paint went on much more evenly on the drywall than it did on the plaster.

5. Drywall is more uniform in size and texture. Because drywall does not have to dry, you can build a wall with it much faster than you could with plaster. This saves time and money.

## CONCRETE SOLUTIONS

One of the biggest problems that ancient engineers faced was how to hold stone or brick structures together. Through trial and error, they discovered that the best way to stack rectangular building materials was to overlap the edges. As the stack rose in height, however, it quickly became unstable and toppled over. What they needed was a way to bind the stones or bricks so that the walls acted like a single unit instead of like a pile of loose blocks.

At first, they tried using a simple mortar made from mud. As the mud dried, it hardened, but it would often crack and quickly wash away when it rained. Later, in Egypt, mortar made from plaster was used. Plaster worked well in the dry, desert environment. However, it too would crack and crumble over time. In wet climates, plaster mortar did not last long because it dissolves quickly in water. The problem was finally solved by Roman engineers. They discovered how to make **cement** using limestone and volcanic ash. When these materials are mixed with water and allowed to dry, they form a solid mass that can hold bricks and stones together. In **Experiment 3:** *Testing Cement Mixtures*, you will mix up several batches of cement to see how they can be put to use in different parts of a structure.

# EXPERIMENT 3

# Testing Cement Mixtures

## Topic

What properties of cement make it a useful building material?

## Introduction

Many building materials are available to architects and engineers today, but the one that is most widely used in modern construction is Portland cement. Even though it is a man-made substance, Portland cement gets its name from a type of natural limestone that can be found on the Isle of Portland in the English Channel. It was patented in 1824 by Joseph Aspdin, a mason from Leeds, England, who was looking for a better type of mortar to hold bricks and stones together.

Portland cement is an artificial mixture containing lime, silica, alumina, and iron oxide. The lime used in the mix generally comes from either crushed limestone, chalk, or in some cases, coral and even seashells. The other components come from different types of clay or crushed shale. After the raw materials are crushed and mixed in the proper proportions, they are heated in a **kiln**, creating a lumpy solid known as cement clinker. This is then ground to make a fine powder, to which gypsum is added. The amount of gypsum helps to control how fast the cement will harden. In this experiment, you will test three cement mixtures to discover some of the special properties of this unique building material.

Plain cement          Cement and sand          Cement and rocks

**Figure 1**

## Time Required

30 minutes to mix, 24 hours drying time, and 15 minutes to test after drying

## Materials

- small bag of Portland cement (available at most home improvement or building supply stores)
- large disposable plastic bowl
- 3 large (16 oz, or 500 mL) disposable plastic cups
- water
- small metal trowel
- 1 cup (250 mL) small pebbles or crushed stone
- 1 cup (250 mL) fine sand
- hammer
- rubber gloves
- heavy work gloves
- dust mask
- goggles or safety glasses
- watch or clock
- waterproof marker (such as a Sharpie)
- newspapers to cover table
- plastic garbage bag
- paper towels
- adult to assist you

> **Safety Note**   During this experiment, you will be working with Portland cement. If wet cement makes contact with skin, it can cause irritation and a burning sensation. Always wear a dust mask, rubber gloves, and safety glasses when mixing the wet cement. If the cement gets on unprotected skin, wash immediately with mild soap and water. If any of the wet cement spills, clean it up immediately with a wet paper towel. It is recommended that you conduct this activity under the supervision of a responsible adult.

## Procedure

1. Spread several layers of newspaper on the table to protect the surface. Put on the dust mask, goggles, and gloves. Place the bowl on the newspapers and use one of the plastic cups to measure ½ cup (125 mL) of dry cement into the bowl. Add about ¼ cup (63 mL) of cold water to the bowl. Use the trowel to stir the cement and water until they are evenly mixed. The mixture should have the consistency of a thick paste. There should be no dry spots, and the mixture should be liquid enough to flow. If necessary, slowly add more water while mixing, but do not make it too runny. Observe the texture of the mixture as you stir. Pour the mixture from the bowl into one of the plastic cups so that it is about ¾ full. Use the marker to label the outside of the cup "cement only." Dump the rest of the mixture from the bowl into the plastic garbage bag and wipe the bowl out with a damp paper towel.

2. Repeat Step 1, only this time in addition to the ½ cup (125 mL) of cement, add ½ cup of fine sand. After the sand and cement have been thoroughly mixed with water, pour the mixture in a second cup and label it "cement and sand." Mix a third batch of cement, but use ½ cup of pebbles or crushed stone instead of sand. After pouring the third mixture into a cup, label it "cement and stone."

3. Place the three cups in a safe location and allow them to dry for 24 hours. Before putting them away, hold each cup briefly in your bare hand and note any temperature differences among them.

4. After 24 hours have passed, test the mixtures in the three cups to make sure that they have dried. If they have, carefully peel away the plastic from the outside and observe the texture of the three mixtures. Put on the goggles and heavy work gloves. Hold the "cement only" mixture in one hand and hit it firmly with the hammer until it cracks. Observe the texture inside. Repeat the same procedure with the other two cups. Compare the hardness of the three mixtures and the way they break. As you observe the three cement mixtures, see if you can recognize where each type of mixture may have been used in and around your home or school.

## Analysis

1. How did the three mixtures feel when you held the cups in your hand before they dried?

2. After the cement dried, how did the texture of the mixtures compare with one another? Which took the most effort to break with the hammer?

3. Based on the appearance of each cement mixture, where do you think that each is commonly used in construction?

 ## What's Going On?

Portland cement is the most common form of hydraulic cement. The term *hydraulic cement* comes from the fact that it must first be mixed with water to activate it. As the cement dries or sets, it forms a solid mass. Hydraulic cement gets it strength from the formation of tiny interlocking crystals that grow as the mixture sets. During the setting process, a chemical reaction takes place and heat is released. As a result, the cups should have felt warm to the touch. This type of reaction is called an exothermic reaction.

Because it can be poured into a mold in its liquid state, Portland cement can be formed into a variety of shapes and can be used in many jobs. Common uses include building foundations, precast pipes, pillars, and posts. It can also be turned into decorative items, such as flowerpots and statues. To give it more strength, Portland cement is often reinforced with steel bars to produce beams and other structural elements for buildings. Large panels of precast, reinforced concrete are used to pave bridge decks and parking garages. Portland cement frequently is mixed with aggregates—such as sand or gravel—for specific uses in construction. When it is mixed with fine sand, it is used as mortar between bricks. When it is mixed with gravel or crushed stone, it is used to make concrete to pave roads and sidewalks.

## Our Findings

1. As the cement began to set, the cups got warm.

2. The plain cement had a smooth texture, the cement with sand was gritty, and the cement with small stones was rough. While they were all difficult to crack with the hammer, the one made from only cement should have been the most difficult to break.

3. The mixture made with only cement is commonly used for columns, pipes, and other structural elements. The mixture made with sand is commonly used as mortar between stones and bricks, and the cement mixed with stone is commonly used for pavement.

## OUT ON THE TARMAC

Concrete is easy to pour, but applying it to a road can be time consuming and expensive. Back in the early 1800s, a Scottish engineer named John McAdam invented another paving technique that also gives us a smooth ride but costs less than cement. The technical name for McAdam's invention is *macadam*, a word that (as you might have guessed) was taken from his name. Macadam roads start out with a compact sublayer of crushed stone. This layer is designed to support the weight of vehicles and people. It is covered with a layer of finer stone, which allows water to drain off to the sides of the road. In modern paving, the road is covered with a top coat of asphalt and hot tar. This binds the stones together and seals the surface. The final product is known as *tarmacadam,* or *tarmac* for short, but it's often referred to as blacktop.

## GETTING STUCK ON GLUE

Glue is the common name for a group of substances that scientists call **adhesives.** The most important property of an adhesive is that it is sticky. This makes it useful to hold or bond things together. In our modern world, adhesives are used in

Originally, tarmac was used extensively to construct runways during World War II. Even though tarless asphalt mixtures have replaced tarmac in many areas, the term is still used to refer to many roads and plane runways.

Typically, the glue applied to an envelope flap is a mixture of water, sugar, starch, and natural gum, called gum arabic, which is produced by the acacia tree.

the manufacturing of thousands of products, including cars, clothing, furniture, appliances, and toys. They also are used to bind books, seal envelopes, and hold postage stamps on letters. Adhesive-backed tape has a wide range of uses, from sealing pipes and ductwork to wrapping packages. Even doctors and dentists use specialized adhesives for closing wounds and putting caps on teeth. In **Experiment 4:** *Making a Simple Adhesive,* you will create a basic glue mixture using some common household substances and then test it to see how effective it is.

# 4

# Making a Simple Adhesive

## Topic

How can milk be turned into glue?

## Introduction

An adhesive or glue is a chemical compound that is used to hold or bond materials together. The earliest recorded use of glue was more than 3,000 years ago in Egypt. Carvings from this time show workers using some type of liquid glue to bond pieces of wood together. Over the centuries, people have learned to make adhesives from a range of materials, including plants, animal bones, and even blood. In this experiment, you are going to make a simple adhesive from milk and then test how effective it is at holding different materials together.

## Time Required

40 minutes to mix, 24 hours drying time, and 15 minutes to test

## Materials

- small saucepan
- stove or hot plate
- fine-mesh strainer
- large bowl
- measuring spoons
- water
- large wooden spoon
- 1 cup (250 mL) nonfat (skim) milk
- white vinegar
- baking soda

- goggles or safety glasses

- watch or clock

- sheet of paper

- index card

- small disposable plastic plate

- small disposable plastic cup

- 2 wooden tongue depressors or popsicle sticks

- 2 pennies

- sink

- adult to assist you

> **Safety Note** During this experiment, you will be heating the milk mixture on a stove or hot plate. It is recommended that you conduct this activity under the supervision of a responsible adult and wear goggles or safety glasses when mixing and pouring the mixture.

## Procedure

1. Pour the milk into the saucepan and stir in 2 tablespoons (30 mL) of white vinegar. Place the saucepan on the stove or hot plate and heat it over low heat while stirring slowly. When solid white clumps appear in the milk, turn off the heat.

2. Place the colander or sieve on top of the large bowl. Carefully pour the milk and vinegar mixture from the saucepan into the colander (see Figure 1) and allow it to drain for about five minutes. After the liquid has drained, use a spoon to transfer the solids back into the saucepan. Pour the liquid from the bowl down the drain and wash the bowl and colander with warm, soapy water.

3. Sprinkle 1 tablespoon (15 mL) of baking soda over the milk solids and stir the mixture. Do NOT heat the mixture this time. As you stir, add water to the mixture a few drops at a time. The solids should start to liquefy. Continue stirring and adding water until the entire mixture is a thick liquid. The glue is now ready to test.

4. Dip the tip of your pointer finger in the glue mixture. Touch it to your thumb and observe how it feels. Wash your fingers and then use the mixture to glue the two tongue depressors together. Also use it to glue the index card to the piece of paper, the two pennies together, and the bottom of the plastic cup to the plastic plate. Allow the glued items to dry for 24 hours and then test them to see how well the glue worked. Try separating the glued items from each other and observe the results.

Saucepan

Vinegar and milk

Strainer

Bowl

**Figure 1**

© Infobase Publishing

## Analysis

1. How did the glue mixture feel when you touched it to your finger?
2. After the glue dried, which items held together best?
3. Based on your experiments, on which materials should you use white glue?

## What's Going On?

The glue that you made in this experiment is commonly called "white glue," and it is one of the most popular adhesives used on paper products and wood. White glue is a casein-based adhesive. Casein is a protein found in milk and milk products, such as cheese, yogurt, and ice cream. When casein comes in contact with an acid, such as vinegar (also called acetic acid), a chemical reaction takes place. The milk begins to curdle, producing lumps. This same process is used in making cheese.

In order for the casein to become an effective adhesive, the acid must first be neutralized, and then it must be turned back into a liquid. Baking soda (also called sodium bicarbonate) is a base, which is the chemical opposite of an acid. When it is mixed with the solid curds, the acid reaction is stopped. Then, adding water causes the solids to dissolve, producing a sticky liquid that can be used to bond materials together.

Casein glue has been used for hundreds of years. It is most effective on porous materials, such as wood and paper. It is not as effective on metals or on smooth, hard plastics. One of the main drawbacks of white glue is that it tends to absorb moisture, causing the bonds to weaken. As a result, it does not work well in damp environments.

## Our Findings

1. The glue felt smooth and sticky.
2. The index card and paper held together best, followed by the tongue depressors. The pennies separated fairly easily, as did the plastic cup from the plastic plate.
3. White glue works best on paper and wood products. It is not as effective on metal and plastic.

## ADVANCED ADHESIVES

For hundreds of years, the only way that people could make adhesives was to start with natural compounds, such as milk, bone, and plants. As scientists developed a better understanding of chemical compounds, they found ways to make adhesives using synthetic compounds. These new compounds enabled scientists to develop adhesives with a wider range of properties and thus many more uses. Today, there are thousands of synthetic adhesives. Some of the most common include thermoplastic adhesives, which can be softened or hardened by changing temperature; contact adhesives, which are based on solvents that evaporate to form strong permanent bonds; pressure-sensitive adhesives, which are commonly used for adhesive tape; and hot-melt adhesives, which contain plastic resins that form rigid bonds when they cool and change phase from liquid to solid.

As scientists developed new and better adhesives, engineers found that these could be used to create new construction materials. One of the most important materials was **plywood.** In **Experiment 5:** ***Putting Plywood to the Test***, you will compare a piece of plywood to a natural wooden board and see what advantages plywood offers in construction.

## EXPERIMENT 5

# Putting Plywood to the Test

## Topic

How does plywood compare to a standard wooden board when it comes to strength and flexibility?

## Introduction

Over the centuries, wood has proved to be an excellent building material. It is strong, and relatively lightweight, compared with stone or brick. In addition, wood can be easily cut and shaped, and pieces can be fastened together using nails and screws. Natural wood does have some drawbacks, however. Because wood is cut from trees, the size of the lumber used for construction is limited by the size of the tree. In addition, natural wood can easily split along the grain. It also can swell and contract as moisture levels change. In an attempt to solve some of these problems, inventors have developed several wood-based building products. One important product is plywood. In this activity, you will compare plywood with natural wood and test to see how plywood solves several of the common problems encountered during construction.

### Time Required

40 minutes

### Materials

- 2 equal-sized bricks
- wood chisel
- hammer
- ruler
- 18 in.-long (45-cm) piece of 1 in. x 6 in. (2.5 cm x 15 cm) pine board

- piece of plywood that is 18 in. (45 cm) long, 6 in. (15 cm) wide, and ⅝ in (15 mm) thick

- goggles

- heavy work gloves

- an adult to assist you

**Safety Note** During this experiment, you will be cutting and splitting wood using a hammer and chisel. Always wear work gloves and safety glasses. It is recommended that you conduct this activity under the supervision of a responsible adult.

## Procedure

1. Closely examine the natural pine board and the piece of plywood. Compare the surface texture and edges of each. Look at the way the grain runs in the natural wood and compare it with the grain in the plywood. Record your observations.

2. Put on the goggles and work gloves. Place the two bricks on a workbench or similar sturdy surface so that they are parallel to each other and about

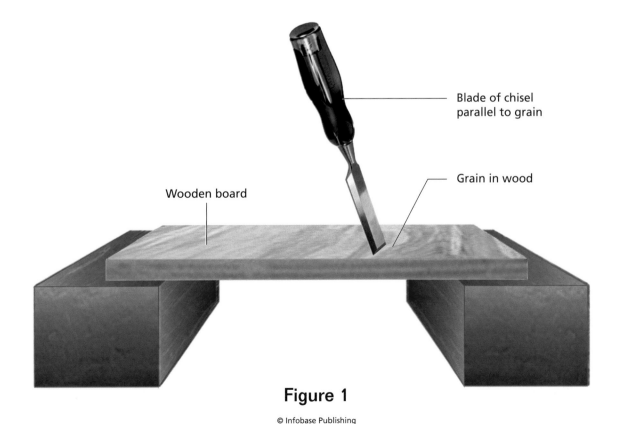

Blade of chisel
parallel to grain

Grain in wood

Wooden board

**Figure 1**

3 in. (7 cm) apart. Place the pine board on top of the bricks so that it bridges the gap between them. The grain of the wood should be parallel to the long axis of the bricks. (See Figure 1.) Strike the center of the board with the hammer several times and observe what happens to the wood. Place the blade of the chisel on the board so that it is running parallel to the grain of the wood. Strike the chisel several times with the hammer and observe what happens to the wood. Record your observations.

3. Remove the pine board from the bricks and replace it with the piece of plywood. Repeat Step 2 using the plywood and record your observations.

## Analysis

1. How did the surface texture and edges of the plywood compare with that of the pine board?

2. How did the grain of the pine board compare with that of the plywood?

3. What happened to the pine board when you hit it with the hammer and then the chisel? How did this compare with the piece of plywood?

4. Based on your observations, what are some of the advantages of using plywood instead of natural wood in construction?

## What's Going On?

Plywood is a manufactured product made from thin layers of wood, or "plies," that have been glued together. Plywood sheets always have an odd number of layers. The outer layers, or "face plies," have the grain running in the same direction. The grain of the inner layers alternates; the next layers in have their grains running in the opposite direction from the face plies. The next layers in have grains running parallel to those of the face plies, and so on. This construction makes a sheet of plywood much stronger than natural lumber because the plywood cannot split along the grain. Alternating the direction of the grain also minimizes the amount of swelling and shrinking from changing moisture conditions. Because plywood sheets are made from smaller pieces of wood glued together, they can be much larger than lumber cut from a single tree. This saves builders time and money when it comes to completing large construction projects.

## Our Findings

1. The pine board was smooth on both faces and along the two uncut edges. The plywood was smooth only on one face, and instead of being a single, solid piece of wood, it was made of several layers of wood joined together.

2. The grain of the pine board ran in the same direction. With the plywood, the grain of the top and bottom layers ran in the same direction, and the grain of the inner layers alternated directions.

3. When the pine board was hit with the hammer, it dented, cracked, and splintered. The outer layer of the plywood chipped, but the board itself bent and bounced back. When the chisel was used on the pine board, the entire piece of wood split along the grain. With the plywood, the chisel only split the top layer.

4. Plywood is much stronger than a piece of natural wood that is the same thickness. Plywood is much less likely than a natural wood board to split and crack under stress.

## PLYWOOD AND PARTICLEBOARD

When modern plywood was first introduced in the early 1900s, it wasn't an immediate success. One of the main problems was that the glues used to bond the plies together weren't waterproof. Once the plywood got wet, the layers started to peel apart. As a result, plywood could not be used outdoors, or in rooms with high moisture levels, such as bathrooms and kitchens. In the mid-1930s, the first reliable waterproof glues were developed. Within a few short years, plywood was being used to cover the outside of buildings as well as their inner walls.

After World War II, much of the United States experienced a boom in new home construction and the demand for all wood products, especially plywood, soared. Mills increased production, but they often struggled to keep up with the demand. Forests were cut down, and new sources of timber were more difficult to find. The increase in production also generated huge amounts of wood waste. In order to combat both problems, the manufactured wood industry hit upon a simple solution: Why not take the waste material and use it to make a building product that could be used in place of wood? That's when **particleboard** was born.

As the name suggests, particleboard is a construction material made from flakes and shavings of wood. They are glued

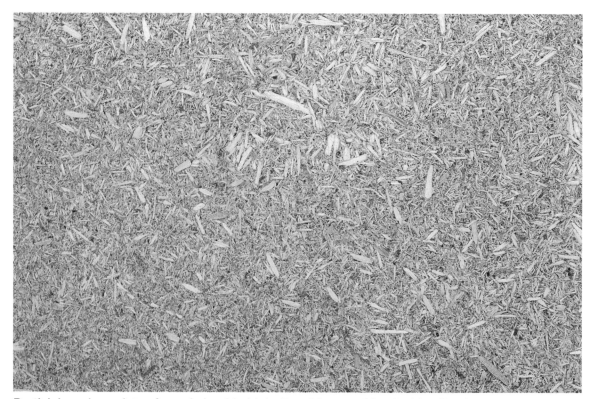

Particleboard consists of wood shredded into tiny chips combined with adhesives.

together to form large sheets, which can be used in place of natural lumber or plywood. In the first step of the manufacturing process, the wood particles are combined with a synthetic binder and a waterproofing agent. The result looks a little like cookie dough. The mixture is heated and pressed into long sheets of different thicknesses. In the final step, the sheets are trimmed and sanded to various sizes and allowed to dry.

## STOPPING HEAT AND COLD

In recent years, one of the biggest concerns with buildings is how much energy they use. Heating buildings in cold weather and cooling them when it is warm consumes a huge amount of energy. Based on estimates by the U.S. Department of Energy, as much as 70% of the energy used in American homes goes for heating and cooling. The main reason for this enormous use of energy is the way heat travels. According to the second law of thermodynamics, heat always travels from a warmer object to a cooler one. On hot days, warm air flows from the outside of a building, heating up the cool air inside. On cold days, the reverse happens: Warm air flows out of the building into the surrounding air. One way to cut down on the flow of heat is to use insulation. Insulating materials are designed to block the movement of heat energy. In **Experiment 6:** *Insulating Properties of Different Materials*, you will test several materials to see which is most effective at reducing the flow of heat.

# Insulating Properties of Different Materials

## Topic

How effective are different materials at insulating against heat loss?

## Introduction

One of the most cost-effective ways of reducing heating and cooling costs in buildings is to use insulation. Insulating materials are designed to reduce the flow of heat energy. In this activity, you will test four materials to see how effective each is at reducing the flow of heat energy. Based on your observations, you will then determine the properties of good insulating materials.

## Time Required

40 minutes

## Materials

- hot plate or stove
- water
- tea kettle or large saucepan
- Pyrex (or other heat-resistant material) measuring cup
- 8 oz (250 mL) Styrofoam hot cup
- 8 oz (250 mL) paper hot cup
- 8 oz (250 mL) ceramic or glass mug
- small, clean, empty metal soup can with label removed
- clear plastic wrap
- 4 large rubber bands
- scissors

- ruler

- small sharp knife

- watch or timer

- 4 identical lab thermometers

- pot holder or oven mitt

- adult to assist you

**Safety Note**   During this experiment you will be heating water and pouring boiling water. It is recommended that you conduct this activity under the supervision of a responsible adult.

## Procedure

1. Fill the tea kettle or saucepan with 4 cups (1,000 mL) of water and heat until it is boiling. While the water is heating, examine the four empty containers. Compare their thicknesses, weights, and the materials from which they are made. Record your observations.

2. Use the scissors to cut four pieces of plastic wrap that are each 5 in. (13 cm) square.

**Figure 1**

3. Once the water starts boiling, turn off the heat and have an adult pour 6 oz (200 mL) of hot water into each of the containers. Immediately cover each container with a piece of plastic wrap and secure the wrap to the container with a rubber band stretched around the top. Cut a small slit in the plastic wrap at the top of each container. Put a lab thermometer into each cup. Figure 1 shows you how this should look. Allow the thermometers to rest in the hot water for one minute. Read each thermometer and record the temperature of each cup on the data table under the heading "Starting Temp."

4. Allow the thermometers to rest in the containers of hot water for five minutes, and record the temperature of each cup again. Follow this procedure every five minutes until a total of 25 minutes has passed. Each time you take a temperature reading, use your hand to feel the outside of the container and record your observations. After taking the final temperature readings, remove the thermometers from the cups and dispose of the water.

| Data Table 1 | | | | |
|---|---|---|---|---|
| | **Paper Cup** | **Styrofoam Cup** | **Ceramic Mug** | **Metal Can** |
| **Description** | | | | |
| | | | | |
| **Starting Temp.** | | | | |
| 5 minutes | | | | |
| 10 minutes | | | | |
| 15 minutes | | | | |
| 20 minutes | | | | |
| 25 minutes | | | | |

## Analysis

1. Which container was heaviest?

2. Which container was the thickest?

3. Which cup felt warmest in your hand after 10 minutes? Which felt coolest?

4. Which cup had the greatest amount of heat loss after 25 minutes?

5. Based on your observations, which material was the best insulator? Which was the worst insulator?

## What's Going On?

The ability of a material to block the flow of heat energy depends on several factors, including its composition and thickness. Most metals are poor insulators because their atomic structure allows energy to rapidly move through them. Metals tend to be excellent conductors of heat, which is why they are used to make pots, pans, and other types of cookware. Glass and ceramic objects also tend to be relatively good conductors, but they offer more resistance to heat flow than metals do. If a piece of glass is thick enough, it can serve as a fairly good insulator. This is why most ceramic coffee mugs tend to be thick and heavy. Most wood—and products made from wood, such as paper—tend to be fairly good insulators as long as they are dry. With wood and paper products, the thicker the material is, the better its insulating properties. Styrofoam is a type of plastic that has exceptionally good insulating properties. Styrofoam is also very lightweight.

When it comes to insulating a building, one of the best techniques is to trap a layer of "dead air" between building materials. Most gases are poor conductors of heat energy. For this reason, most modern insulating windows have two layers of glass with a layer of air or some other gas filling the space between them. Other insulating materials include fiberglass and cellulose fill. Like Styrofoam, both of these contain many air spaces between the solid particles. One way of determining how effective a particular material is at insulating a building is to look at its R-value. This number is a measure of the thermal resistance of heat flow. The higher a material's R-value is, the better it will be at insulating a structure.

## Our Findings

1. The ceramic mug was the heaviest.

2. The Styrofoam cup and ceramic mug were about the same thickness.

3. The metal can was the warmest to the touch, while the Styrofoam was the coolest.

4. The metal can had the greatest heat loss.

5. The Styrofoam cup was the best insulator, and the metal can was the worst. The paper cup and ceramic mug were in the middle.

## BUILDING THE FUTURE

Scientists and engineers are working hard to come up with new and improved building materials that require less energy and materials to make, and that also save energy in the structures in which they are used. In many cases, the best solution involves the recycling of old building products. This saves energy and reduces construction and demolition waste. One material that has a long history of being recycled is metal. In the next chapter, we will explore the history and uses of metal and how this natural substance has been modified to become one of the most important man-made materials on the planet.

# 2

# Magnificent Metals

Metals are some of the most important materials found in the modern world. Like stone and wood, metals are naturally occurring substances that people discovered in the environment. At first, metals were used only in their native or natural forms. Over time, individuals found that they could

This close-up of iron pyrite shows its shine. The mineral's metallic luster and brassy color make it look gold, which has earned it the nickname of "fool's gold."

modify many of the properties of metals by heating them, hammering them, and combining them with other chemical elements. Today, when it comes to the development of new man-made materials, the science of metallurgy is one of the most important fields. In **Experiment 7:** *Properties of Metals*, you will compare a small steel rod to a piece of wood to discover some of the special properties that make metals so magnificent to work with.

EXPERIMENT

**7**

# Properties of Metals

## Topic

What are some of the unique properties of metals?

## Introduction

Scientists use the word *metal* to describe a class of chemical elements that have a unique set of properties. Some typical metals include iron, copper, silver, tin, and gold. Today, metals are used for thousands of jobs, from making tools and building bridges to providing electrical wiring and plumbing in houses. You can find metals at work in the kitchen, garage, and even the bathroom. In this activity, you will compare similar-sized pieces of metal and wood to see how their properties are different.

## Time Required

40 minutes

## Materials

- wire coat hanger

- 3 thin wooden or bamboo barbecue skewers

- pliers or wire cutter

- ruler

- 2 pieces of insulated bell wire with ends stripped, each about 12 in. (30 cm) long

- "D" battery

- 1.5-volt LED (available at an electronics store)

- candle

- cellophane tape

- matches or lighter

- ceramic or glass plate

- watch or timer

- pair of work gloves

- adult to assist you

**Safety Note** During this experiment, you will be working with sharp cutting tools and an open flame. It is recommended that you conduct this activity under the supervision of a responsible adult.

## Procedure

1. Remove all the paper or cardboard from the coat hanger. Put on the work gloves and use the wire cutters or pliers to cut three straight sections that are each 6 in. (15 cm) long. Cut the three wooden barbecue skewers to the same length as the pieces of coat hanger.

2. Hold one metal rod in your two hands by the ends. Slowly bend it so that the ends touch. Do the same thing with one of the wooden rods. Observe what happens to each rod when you bend it.

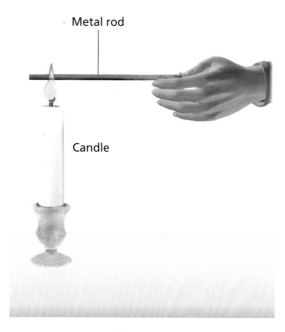

**Figure 1**

3. Remove the gloves and have an adult light the candle. Hold one end of a wooden rod directly in the flame for about 15 seconds. (See Figure 1.) Observe what happens to the rod and how the rod feels in your fingers. If the rod should catch fire, blow it out and place it on the glass plate. Repeat the procedure with a metal rod and observe the differences between the metal rod and the wooden rod.

4. Take the two pieces of wire and twist one end of each wire around one of the metal leads coming from the LED. The two wires should then be connected to the LED. Tape the bare end of one of the wires to the (-) end of the battery. Hold the bare end of the second wire against the (+) end of the battery. The LED should light. Remove the wire from the (+) end of the battery and twist the bare end around one end of the last metal rod. Touch the free end of the metal rod to the (+) end of the battery. (See Figure 2.) Observe what happens. Remove the metal rod and repeat the same procedure with the last wooden rod. Observe what happens.

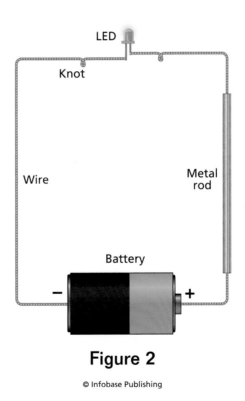

**Figure 2**

© Infobase Publishing

## Analysis

1. What happened to the metal rod when you bent it in your hands? How did this compare with the wooden rod?

2. How did the metal rod feel after you held the end in the flame for 15 seconds? How did this compare with the wooden rod?

3. What happened to the LED when you used the metal rod to connect it to the battery? What happened when you used the wooden rod?

## What's Going On?

Metals have unique properties that make them useful in our modern world. Most metals are **ductile**, which means that they can be twisted and bent into a variety of shapes without breaking. This property makes it possible to draw a piece of metal out into a thin wire or shape it into a pipe for carrying liquids. Most metals are good conductors, which means that heat energy can flow through them. Cookware often is made from metal, as are barbecue grills. Though some metals, such as lead and gold, melt at a relatively low temperatures, most metals do not burn (oxidize) until the temperature is very high. This makes them ideal for use as protective coverings for devices that have an open flame. Most metals also are good conductors of electricity. As a result, they can be used to make wires and other electrical components.

## Our Findings

1. The metal rod bent easily, while the wooden rod snapped.
2. The end of the metal rod that you were holding got warm, but the end that was in the flame did not burn. The end of the wooden rod that you were holding did not get warm, but the end that was in the flame caught on fire.
3. The LED lit up when it was connected to the battery with the metal rod, but did not light when it was connected to the wooden rod.

## MAN-MADE METALS

At first, the metals that people used to make tools and works of art were in their native form. These metals included copper, gold, silver, and even a small amount of iron, in some cases, which came from meteorites that crashed into the Earth.

Most metals do not occur as pure elements. Instead, they are usually found as **ores**, combined with other minerals in rocks. Before the metal in an ore can be used, it must be separated from the other minerals and purified. The most common way of separating a metal from its ore is by smelting. This process usually involves crushing the ore and heating the material to a high temperature. The metal generally melts at a lower temperature than the surrounding minerals do. Once the metal is in a liquid state, it can be poured off and cooled, producing ingots (molds in which metal is cast) of relatively pure metal.

The ability to heat metal to higher temperatures led to the production of **alloys**. Alloys are combinations of two or more

Molten bronze is poured into casts at the American Fine Arts Foundry in Burbank, California, for statues to be given away at the 2010 Screen Actors Guild Awards.

metals, or mixtures of a metal with another substance in a molten (melted) state. Making alloys allowed people to create new metals with different properties. One of the first alloys created was bronze, a combination of copper and tin. Bronze is harder than pure copper, and it holds a much sharper edge, making it better suited for swords and knives. Today, most of the metals we use are alloys. One of the most important is steel, an alloy of iron and at least one other chemical element. Unlike most metals, iron has a unique property that allows it to be easily separated from other materials: It is magnetic. In **Experiment 8:** *Magnetic Properties of Steel*, you will use this property to test some of the alloys of iron to see if they are magnetic, too.

# EXPERIMENT 8

# Magnetic Properties of Steel

## Topic

Are all alloys of iron magnetic?

## Introduction

The first person to report on the force of magnetism was Greek philosopher Thales. Around 600 B.C., he noticed that certain heavy, black rocks had a strange attraction for each other. Almost 2,200 years later, English physician William Gilbert discovered that pieces of iron could be magnetized if they were brought in contact with another magnet. An iron bar can be magnetized because of the behavior of the electrons that are found in its atoms. When the element iron is mixed with other elements to make steel, some of its magnetic properties change. In this activity, you will test several types of steel to see how their magnetic properties vary.

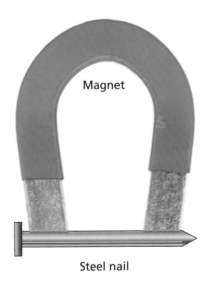

Magnet

Steel nail

**Figure 1**

© Infobase Publishing

## Time Required

30 minutes

## Materials

- strong magnet
- steel nail
- penny
- dime or quarter
- aluminum soda can
- clean, empty, steel soup or tuna fish can
- galvanized steel washer (available at a hardware store)
- piece of stainless-steel cutlery (butter knife or spoon)
- several pieces of stainless-steel cookware (pots, pans, colander)
- object made of painted steel (refrigerator, stove)

**Safety Note** No special safety precautions are needed for this activity. Please review and follow the safety guidelines before proceeding.

## Procedure

1. Touch the magnet to each of the metal objects. Based on how well the magnet sticks, rate the attraction as strong, weak, or none. Select several other metal objects from around your home or classroom and test them using the magnet as well. Record the information on the data table. Use your observations to answer the questions in the analysis section.

| Data Table 1 | |
|---|---|
| **Item** | **Type of Magnetic Attraction** |
| Steel nail | |
| Aluminum soda can | |
| Penny | |

| | |
|---|---|
| Quarter | |
| Steel food can | |
| Painted steel | |
| Galvanized washer | |
| Stainless-steel cutlery | |
| Stainless-steel cookware | |
| Other items (list your own): | |
| | |
| | |
| | |
| | |

## Analysis

1. Which items were strongly attracted to the magnet?
2. Which items showed no attraction to the magnet?
3. Did paint have any effect on the magnetic attraction of a piece of steel?
4. How did the magnetic attraction of the stainless-steel items compare with the other steel items?
5. Which of the items that you selected were magnetic?

### What's Going On?

A magnet's ability to be attracted to a piece of steel depends on the mixture of chemical elements used to make the steel. It does not depend on whether the steel is coated with paint or another metal. Galvanized steel is steel that has been plated with the metal zinc. Most steel food cans are plated with tin. In most cases, these materials still exhibit magnetic properties, because the magnet is attracted to the steel beneath the other metal. It is only when the composition of the steel changes that its magnetic properties will change.

The invention of steel was probably an accidental discovery that came about when some carbon from charcoal fires used to smelt iron got mixed with the iron itself. The result was a metal that was much stronger and harder than pure iron. Over the years, the steelmaking process has been refined to produce a range of alloys with specific properties. Most of the steel used in building and bridge construction, and in the manufacturing of appliances (such as refrigerators, stoves, and toaster ovens), is considered to be "low-alloy" steel. This type of steel is made mostly of iron, and is usually less than 5% other metals or elements. High-alloy steel contains more than 5% of at least one other metal.

Stainless steel is a high-alloy steel, which contains at least 10.5% chromium, in addition to varying amounts of nickel. Stainless steel is made to resist **corrosion** and **rust**, which is often a problem with low-alloy steel. Stainless steel also is resistant to heat; this is why it often is used in the manufacturing of cookware and cutlery. The ability of stainless steel to attract a magnet depends on the amount of chromium and nickel used in the mixture. The most basic form of stainless steel is made from iron, carbon, and chromium. This mixture is called martensitic stainless steel, and is generally used in cutlery. It is usually magnetic. The more common form of stainless steel is called austenitic stainless steel, which is either slightly magnetic or nonmagnetic. This type has a much higher nickel content, which changes the internal arrangement of the atoms in the alloy, making it less magnetic.

## Our Findings

1. The steel nail, food can, galvanized washer, and painted metal all should have been strongly attracted to the magnet.
2. The aluminum can, penny, and quarter all should have shown no attraction to the magnet.
3. The painted steel still should have been attracted to the magnet.
4. The stainless-steel items will show varying degrees of attraction to a magnet, ranging from a strong attraction to none at all.
5. The materials that you selected will have varying degrees of magnetism depending on what they are made of.

## TARNISH, CORROSION, AND RUST

Over time, items made from metal tend to change when they are exposed to water and air. In some cases, the changes are minor. When a piece of silver jewelry is new, it is bright and shiny. After a while, the surface will turn dull gray, or even black. When this happens, we say that the silver has tarnished. The problem can be quickly solved with a little polish and some rubbing with a cloth. With a steel bridge, however, exposure to moist air can be much more destructive. In this case, instead of simply changing color, the surface of the steel begins to rust. If it is left untreated, the rust will weaken the steel to the point where the bridge could collapse.

Both tarnish and rust fall under the heading of a chemical process known as corrosion. All metals are subject to the affects of corrosion, but do all metals corrode at the same rate? In **Experiment 9:** *Corrosion Rates of Different Metals*, you are going to test four metal objects to see how resistant each is to the effects of corrosion. In **Experiment 10:** *Removing Corrosion from Copper*, you will test several methods for cleaning copper pennies and determine which is the most effective at removing corrosion.

Soaking pennies in acid removes oxidation and restores the pennies to their original color and shine.

# EXPERIMENT 9

# Corrosion Rates of Different Metals

## Topic

Do all metals corrode at the same rate?

## Introduction

Metals tend to react with chemicals in the environment. This often leads to the surface of the metal changing through a process known as corrosion. Water is one common compound that causes corrosion in metals. In this experiment, you will test the corrosion resistance of four metal objects when each is allowed to react with water for several days.

## Time Required

20 minutes preparation, 5 days to observe reactions

## Materials

- piece of plain steel wool (without soap)
- steel paper clip
- small piece of aluminum foil
- brass paper fastener
- water
- pliers
- plastic fork
- 4 small (8 oz, or 200 mL) disposable plastic cups

---

**Safety Note**   No special safety precautions are needed for this activity. **Please review and follow the safety guidelines before proceeding.**

## Procedure

1. Observe the four metal objects and record their appearances on the data table under the heading "Day 1." Place one object in the bottom of each plastic cup and fill each cup half full with water. In order to keep the aluminum foil from floating to the surface, you will have to roll it into a small ball and squeeze it tightly between the jaws of the pliers.

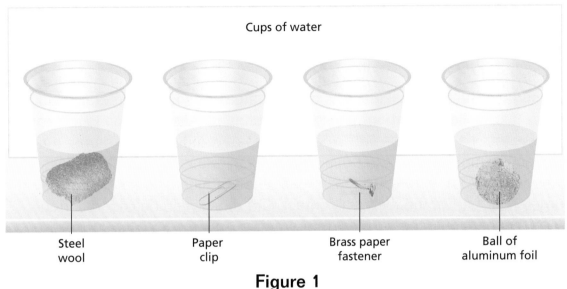

Cups of water

Steel
wool

Paper
clip

Brass paper
fastener

Ball of
aluminum foil

**Figure 1**

© Infobase Publishing

2. Wait for 24 hours to pass and remove the objects from the cups using the plastic fork. Observe each of the objects and record the observations on the data table under the heading "Day 2." Return each item to its cup.

3. Repeat Step 2 three more times until five days have passed. Record your observations in the appropriate places on the data chart. Answer the questions based on your observations.

| Data Table 1 | | | | |
|---|---|---|---|---|
| | **Steel Wool** | **Steel Paper Clip** | **Brass Fastener** | **Aluminum Foil** |
| Day 1 | | | | |
| Day 2 | | | | |
| Day 3 | | | | |
| Day 4 | | | | |
| Day 5 | | | | |

## Analysis

1. Which metal showed the most corrosion?

2. Which metal corroded the least?

3. How did the reaction of the steel paper clip compare to the reaction of the steel wool?

4. Based on your experiment, why do most beverage makers use aluminum cans instead of steel cans for packaging their products?

## What's Going On?

The chemical reaction that produces corrosion in metals is called **oxidation**. What's interesting is that oxidation is the same process that happens in a fire. When a piece of wood or paper burns, the oxidation is rapid, and a great deal of energy is released. Scientists call this combustion. With metals, oxidation reactions are much slower. Instead of burning, the part of the metal in contact with the oxygen begins to corrode. When this happens, the surface of the metal becomes dull and often will change color. In some cases, the metal will eventually disintegrate and fall apart.

Metals have different levels of resistance to corrosion. Pure gold is extremely resistant to corrosion. This is one reason why it is so valuable. In addition to being used in jewelry and works of fine art, gold is used for electronic connections in places where failure due to corrosion cannot happen, such as the space shuttle. In this experiment, we saw that the metals corroded at different rates. The aluminum appeared to change the least, while the steel wool corroded the most. The brass changed very little, but there should have been a color change. Both the paper clip and steel wool rusted, but the steel wool corroded faster because it had a greater surface area than the paper clip. The increased surface area allows more oxidation to take place between the metal and the water.

## Our Findings

1. The steel showed the most corrosion.

2. The aluminum foil showed the least corrosion.

3. Even though they were both made of steel, the steel wool corroded faster than the paper clip.

4. Aluminum is more resistant to corrosion than steel, which means that beverages will last longer in aluminum cans.

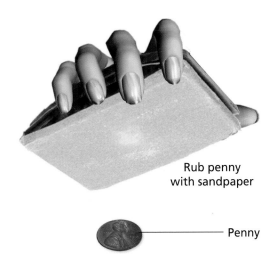 **EXPERIMENT 10** ## Removing Corrosion from Copper

## Topic

What is the most effective way of removing corrosion from copper pennies?

## Introduction

When an object made of copper is exposed to the element oxygen, it undergoes a chemical change on its surface. This forms a new substance called copper oxide. Copper oxide makes the object look dull and dirty. In this experiment, you will use pennies to test whether substances can corrode copper or remove corrosion from it.

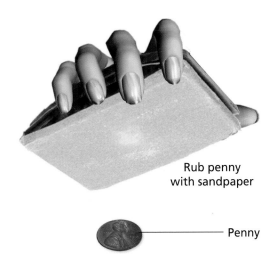

Rub penny
with sandpaper

Penny

**Figure 1**

© Infobase Publishing

 ## Time Required

20 minutes preparation, 2 hours to observe reaction

 ## Materials

- 5 dull, tarnished pennies

- water

- small piece of sandpaper

- dishwashing liquid

- 2 plastic teaspoons

- table salt

- ½ cup (125 mL) lemon juice

- 2 small disposable plastic cups

- 2 paper towels

- timer or watch

- marker

**Safety Note** No special safety precautions are needed for this activity. Please review and follow the safety guidelines before proceeding.

## Procedure

1. Observe the tarnished pennies. Rub the back of one penny several times with a piece of sandpaper. See how the back of the penny now looks, compared with the front of the penny. Record your observations.

2. Fill one of the plastic cups about half full with water and add 1 teaspoon (5 mL) of dishwashing liquid. Stir the mixture until it produces bubbles. Place two pennies in the cup and allow them to soak undisturbed for 10 minutes.

3. Fill the second cup half full with lemon juice and add 1 teaspoon (5mL) of salt. Stir the mixture until the salt dissolves. Place the last two pennies in the cup with the lemon juice and allow them to soak undisturbed for 10 minutes.

4. Remove the two pennies from the cup with the dishwashing liquid and rinse them with water. Observe the pennies and compare them with how they looked before they soaked in the solution. Record your observations.

5. After 10 minutes, remove the two pennies from the lemon juice solution. Rinse one thoroughly with water and place it on a paper towel labeled "rinsed." Place the second penny, **without rinsing it**, directly on a paper towel labeled "not rinsed." Observe the two pennies and compare them with how they looked before you soaked them in the lemon juice solution.

6. Allow the two pennies that had soaked in the lemon juice solution to sit undisturbed on the paper towels for 24 hours and then observe them again. Compare the two pennies and record your observations.

## Analysis

1. How did the surface of the penny that you rubbed with the sandpaper compare with the surface that was not rubbed?

2. What happened to the surfaces of the two pennies that soaked in the dishwashing liquid?

3. What happened to the surfaces of the two pennies that soaked in the lemon juice solution?

4. After 24 hours, how did the surface of the penny that was rinsed compare with the surface of the penny that was not rinsed?

### What's Going On?

In our modern world, one of the biggest challenges that we face is how to keep metal objects looking shiny and new. Everything from fine silverware to brass doorknobs will tarnish and corrode over time. Unlike dirt and grime, corrosion cannot be washed off with detergent or soap. In this experiment, you saw that pennies that soaked in dishwashing liquid still looked dull when they were removed from the water. In order to restore the shiny look to the surface of a corroded copper object, the layer of copper oxide has to be removed. Rubbing the metal with an abrasive material—such as sandpaper or emery cloth—will do the job, but it can also leave scratches. A safer way to remove the corrosion is to soak a tarnished copper object in an acidic solution. Acids are chemicals that have extra hydrogen ions (an ion is an atom that has an electric charge). The hydrogen ions react with the oxygen in the copper oxide to form water and pure copper. In this experiment, the lemon juice and salt solution was the acid.

After the copper oxide is removed from the surface of the pennies, they look bright and shiny again. Rinsing off the acid and salt stops the reaction. If the lemon juice and salt solution is allowed to dry on the surface of a penny, however, the penny soon will begin to turn green. This is due to a second chemical reaction taking place. The copper atoms combine with the chlorine in the salt and oxygen in the air to form a new compound called malachite. Probably the most famous example of this chemical reaction can be seen on the Statue of Liberty, which is covered with copper sheeting that has turned green. Malachite often can be seen covering the copper roofs and downspouts of many older buildings, especially if they are located near salt water.

## Our Findings

1. The sandpaper removed some of the tarnish from the surface of the penny, revealing shiny copper underneath.

2. There was little if any change to the surface of the pennies that soaked in dishwashing liquid. Soap did not remove the tarnish.

3. The lemon juice solution removed most of the tarnish from the surface of the pennies, revealing bright, shiny copper.

4. After 24 hours, the penny that had soaked in the lemon juice solution and was rinsed with water remained shiny, while the unrinsed penny developed a greenish coating.

## FEELING RUSTY

From the time that people first started making tools and structures out of iron, one of the biggest problems they faced was how to keep them from rusting away. Given enough time and the right conditions, almost any type of metal will corrode or oxidize. With metals such as aluminum or zinc, the oxidation layer on the surface of the metal actually helps protect the underlying material from further corrosion. This is because the oxide layer is insoluble in water; once it forms, it stays attached to the metal.

Iron-based metals are different. The technical name for rust is iron oxide trihydrate. When a piece of iron or steel rusts, the iron oxide layer that forms on the surface of the metal is water

This August 2007 image shows a rusty gusset plate on the Interstate 35W bridge, which collapsed in Minneapolis, Minnesota. Gusset plates were originally attached with rivets—old technology that is more likely to slip than the bolts used in modern bridges. Gussets are also weakened and thinned by years of welding.

soluble. If the rusting piece of metal is soaking in water, the oxide layer slowly dissolves away. If the rusting piece of metal is exposed to the air, pieces of iron oxide begin to flake off. In either case, the underlying metal gets weaker over time. As you can imagine, this could create serious problems for a bridge or other structure made from steel. As it turns out, where a piece of steel is located plays a big role in how fast it will rust. In **Experiment 11:** *Environmental Factors Affecting Rust,* you will test to see the conditions under which a piece of steel will corrode quickly.

# EXPERIMENT 11

# Environmental Factors Affecting Rust

## Topic

Which conditions cause steel to rust quickly?

## Introduction

If you have ever accidentally left your bike out in the rain, you know how quickly rust can form on unprotected surfaces, such as chains and gears. Rust can form wherever untreated iron or steel is left exposed, but the rate of the oxidation depends on the environment in which the metal is found. In this activity, you are going to test four situations to see which will cause a piece of steel to rust the fastest.

## Time Required

20 minutes preparation, 5 days of observation

## Materials

- 4 rust-free steel paper clips
- 4 small (8 oz, or 250 mL) disposable plastic cups
- water
- plastic teaspoon
- white vinegar
- table salt
- cooking oil (baby oil will work, too)
- permanent marker

| **Safety Note** No special safety precautions are needed for this activity. Please review and follow the safety guidelines before proceeding. |
| --- |

## Procedure

1. Observe the paper clips. Make certain that they are free from any rust or tarnish. Use the permanent marker to label the cups "plain water," "salt water," "vinegar," and "oil." Place one paper clip in the bottom of each plastic cup.

2. Fill the cup labeled "plain water" about half full with ordinary tap water. Do the same to the cup labeled "salt water" and then add 2 teaspoons (10 mL) of table salt. Stir the mixture until all the salt dissolves. Fill the cup labeled "oil" half full with oil, and fill the cup labeled "vinegar" half full with white vinegar. Place the cups in a secure location, where they can sit undisturbed for several days.

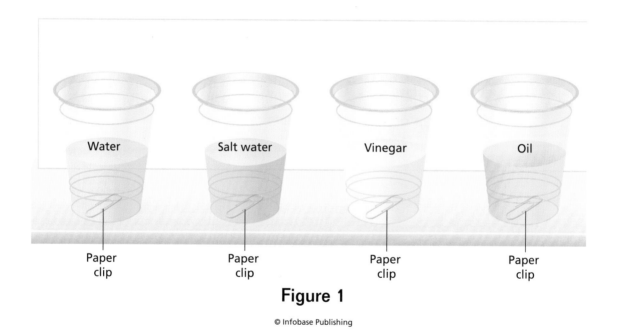

**Figure 1**

© Infobase Publishing

3. After 24 hours have passed, observe the paper clip in each cup and record the observations on the data table. Repeat this procedure for three more days until a total of five days have passed. Use your observations to answer the questions.

| Data Table 1 | | | | |
|---|---|---|---|---|
| | **Plain Water** | **Salt Water** | **Vinegar** | **Oil** |
| Day 2 | | | | |
| Day 3 | | | | |
| Day 4 | | | | |
| Day 5 | | | | |

## Analysis

1. Under which conditions did the paper clip rust fastest?
2. Which condition produced no rust on the paper clip?
3. Based on your observations, which do you think would rust faster, an iron bridge over an ocean inlet or one over a freshwater river?
4. Based on your observations, why is it a good idea to oil your bicycle chain and gears periodically?
5. Based on your observations, what effects might acid rain have on structures made from untreated iron or steel?

### What's Going On?

The rate at which iron oxide forms on a piece of steel is controlled by many factors, including the chemistry of the surrounding environment. Before a piece of steel can rust, a chemical change must occur within the iron atoms found in the steel. The iron atoms become iron *ions*. An ion is an atom that has gained or lost electrons. Instead of being electrically neutral, an ion has a positive or negative charge. It's this charge that allows the iron ions to react with the oxygen to form iron oxide, or rust. When iron and steel soak in ordinary water, the iron atoms ionize slowly, so rust will appear over time.

When salt is added to water, the ionization process speeds up. As a result, objects made from iron and steel tend to rust faster near the ocean, where they can come into contact with salt spray. This is also why cars rust faster when they are driven in areas that use road salt to melt ice in the winter.

In addition to salt, acids also help to speed up the ionization process. Another name for vinegar is acetic acid. This is why the paper clip that was soaking in the vinegar also rusted quickly. Unlike salt water and acid, most oil tends to slow or even stop the ionization process. As a result, the paper clip that soaked in oil did not rust at all. One way to protect untreated steel from rusting quickly is to coat it in oil or grease.

## Our Findings

1. The paper clip in the vinegar should have rusted the quickest.
2. The paper clip in the oil should not have rusted at all.
3. The bridge over salt water would tend to rust faster than the one over fresh water.
4. Oil will help to reduce friction and reduce the amount of rust forming.
5. Acid precipitation generally increases the rate of corrosion of steel.

## STOPPING RUST

Over the years, scientists and engineers have tried to come up with a variety of ways to keep iron and steel from rusting. As you discovered in the previous experiment, coating steel in oil or grease is the simplest way to keep it from oxidizing. This method works well for gears, chains, and other mechanical parts that benefit from lubrication, but having a grease-covered doorknob or faucet would pose a bit of a problem.

A second way to combat the effects of corrosion of bare metal is to paint it. In most cases, even a thin layer of paint creates a barrier between the reactive surface of the metal and chemicals in the environment. This helps slow the rate of oxidation. However, paint does not stop corrosion. Eventually, the metal underneath will begin to oxidize, especially where the paint is chipped or scratched. Once this happens, the paint will begin to flake, and rust will run rampant. This is especially true on bridges and ships exposed to salt water. As a result, they have to be scraped and painted on a regular basis.

In the 1700s, advances in chemistry and the discovery of a new form of electricity finally gave engineers a more permanent solution to the problem of corrosion. In **Experiment 12: *Electroplating Metal***, you will use a battery and a piece of copper to discover for yourself how this special technique works.

# EXPERIMENT 12 Electroplating Metal

## Topic

How can one type of metal be coated with another type of metal?

## Introduction

Electroplating is a technique that uses an electric current to deposit one type of metal directly onto the surface of another metal. The two metals are placed in a chemical solution with an electric current running through it. Jewelry is often electroplated with gold or silver to make it more valuable, and steel is electroplated with zinc or tin to prevent it from rusting and corroding. In this activity, you are going to electroplate a steel nail with copper to see how the process works.

## Time Required

60 minutes

## Materials

- U.S. penny minted before 1982
- U.S. penny minted after 1982
- large steel nail
- 6-volt lantern battery
- 2 cups (500 mL) white vinegar
- clean 1-lb (0.45-kg) disposable plastic deli container
- salt
- paper towel
- plastic teaspoon

- 2 pieces of insulated copper wire, each about 12 in. (30 cm) long

- wire strippers

- fine sandpaper

- hammer

- wooden block

- sturdy table

- goggles or safety glasses

- adult to assist you

> **Safety Note**    During this experiment, you will be punching a hole in a penny with a nail. Be certain to wear safety glasses. It is recommended that you conduct this activity under the supervision of a responsible adult.

## Procedure

1. Observe the two pennies. Deeply scratch the surface of both pennies with the nail. Observe the differences in the metals below the scratches. Rub the shaft of the nail and the front and back of the pre-1982 penny several times with sandpaper to remove any rust or corrosion. Clean the surfaces with a damp paper towel. Place the wooden block on top of a sturdy table and put the pre-1982 penny on top of it. Put on the safety glasses. Then, using the nail and hammer, have an adult punch a hole through the penny.

2. Pour the vinegar into the plastic container and stir in 4 teaspoons (20 mL) of salt until it dissolves. Use the wire strippers to remove about 1 in. (2 cm) of insulation from both ends of the two pieces of wire. Wrap one bare end of one wire around the head of the nail and loop one bare end of the other wire through the hole in the penny. Bend the wire so that it does not slip out of the hole.

3. Attach the other end of the wire that is attached to the penny to the positive (+) terminal of the battery. Attach the other end of the wire attached to the nail to the negative (-) terminal of the battery. Submerge the wired penny in the vinegar solution. Place the nail with the wire attached in the solution so that only the bottom half of the nail is submerged. The setup should look like Figure 1.

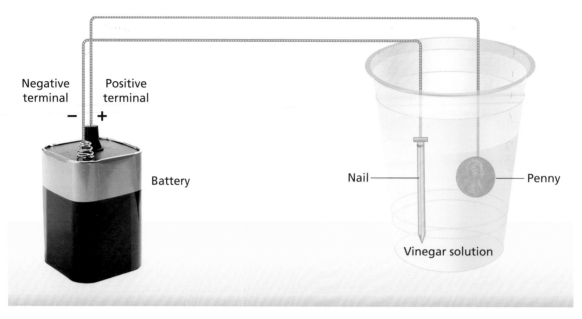

**Figure 1**

© Infobase Publishing

4. Observe what happens to the vinegar when you place the two objects in the solution. Allow the nail and penny to rest in the vinegar solution for about 45 minutes. Then disconnect the wires from the battery and carefully observe the surface of the nail and the penny. Record your observations.

## Analysis

1. How did the metal in the two pennies compare where you scratched them?
2. What happened to the vinegar solution near the nail when you connected the battery and submerged the two objects?
3. After 45 minutes, how did the end of the nail that was soaking in the solution compare with the end of the nail that was out of the solution?
4. What happened to the surface of the penny after it was submerged in the solution?

## What's Going On?

The plating of one metal on top of another is common today. "Galvanized" steel has a layer of zinc on top of it to slow rust and corrosion. The same is true for tin-plated steel food cans and chrome-plated car bumpers. In this experiment, you used an electric current to transfer copper metal from the penny to the surface of the steel nail. This process is called electroplating. Electroplating works due to the movement of electrons through the vinegar solution when the battery is connected to the two metal objects. Vinegar is a type of acid called acetic acid. When salt is added to the vinegar, it dissolves, separating into charged atoms called ions. This type of solution is a very good conductor of electricity and is called an electrolyte solution.

When an electric current flows through an electrolyte solution, electrons move from the negative terminal (cathode) toward the positive terminal (anode). Because the penny is attached to the positive terminal of the battery, it serves as the anode. The nail is the cathode. When the current flows through the penny, the copper atoms lose some of their electrons and become positively charged ions. Some of these copper ions dissolve into the electrolyte solution and are attracted to the surface of the negatively charged nail. When the copper ions reach the surface of the nail, they are turned back into copper atoms and begin to coat the surface of the nail with copper. The longer the current flows through the electroplating device, the more copper is deposited on the nail. In the process, the copper penny loses some metal from its surface, exposing fresh copper underneath. This is why the penny begins to look bright and shiny.

## Our Findings

1. The penny that was newer than 1982 had a gray metal under a copper-colored coating. The pre-1982 penny was copper throughout.
2. The solution began to bubble.
3. The end of the nail that was submerged in the solution was copper colored, and the end that was in the air was silver-gray.
4. The surface of the penny became bright and clean.

## MAKING MODERN METAL MONEY

One of the most common places to see copper-plated metal is in modern U.S. pennies. Originally, pennies were made from pure copper, but from 1864 to 1962, pennies were made from a copper alloy called bronze, which contained a small amount of tin. Due to a shortage of copper during World War II, the 1943 penny was made of zinc-coated steel. This has made it a favorite of coin collectors. In 1944, pennies were again made from bronze until 1962. Then, the decision was made to remove the tin from pennies, so the composition changed to an alloy made from 95% copper and 5% zinc. This continued until the early 1980s. At this time, the cost of copper became so great that the amount of copper used in a penny actually cost more than a penny. This financial problem led to a decision to greatly reduce the copper content of the penny. To keep the same look of the copper-colored penny, mint managers made the new pennies from copper-plated zinc. If you scratch the surface of a modern penny, you will see the silver-gray zinc underneath.

## GALVANIC CURRENT AND BUILDING BATTERIES

In the late 1700s, a growing understanding of the chemical properties of metals led scientists to make a discovery that changed the course of history. As the result of some "dumb luck" and some careful observations, electricity became a useful source of energy. People have known about electricity for quite some time. As far back as 600 B.C., a philosopher named Thales of Miletus reported on its mysterious properties. The type of electricity that Thales dealt with is called static electricity. It makes your socks stick together in the dryer and gives you a shock when you walk across a carpet and touch a doorknob. For more than 2,000 years, static was the only type of electricity that scientists knew about. That all changed with the work of two Italian scientists, Luigi Galvani and Alessandro Volta. Their work with "animal electricity" would lead to the discovery of electrical current and the invention of the battery.

Luigi Galvani was a scientist whose primary interest was in the anatomy and physiology of animals. In the process of dissecting frogs, he noticed that whenever the leg muscle was given a static shock, the severed leg of the frog would twitch. He then took it a step further and showed that the same type of reaction would happen when the frog's leg was suspended from

A machine operator fills a hopper with unstamped pennies at the U.S. Mint in Philadelphia, Pennsylvania.

Alessandro Volta shows his electic battery to French leader Napoleon Bonaparte and members of the Institut de France in 1801.

copper hook connected to an iron railing. He reasoned that the cause of this twitching action was some type of "animal electricity" found in all living things.

Galvani published his findings in 1791, and they were read by Volta. Volta disagreed with Galvani's idea of animal electricity and began conducting his own experiments. By 1799, he was able to show that the frog leg twitched because the two metals were creating some type of electricity that caused the muscle to contract. In 1800, he built the first electrochemical cell from metal disks and felt soaked in an acid solution. His "voltaic pile" was the forerunner of the modern battery. Today, you can't even talk about electricity without mentioning Volta's name: The "volt" is the unit used to measure the amount of electric pressure in a circuit. Galvani also is remembered because the electricity produced by two dissimilar metals connected by an electrolyte is called galvanic current.

# Polymers and Plastics

Take a look around you. How many things can you find that are made of **plastic**? The number of objects is probably pretty large. It doesn't matter where you are. From kitchen utensils and food packages to the clothes we wear and cars we drive, many things are made from plastic. In fact, these days it's difficult to find things that don't have plastics in them. It's hard to imagine that less than 200 years ago, none of these materials existed. Plastics are one of the most important examples of man-made materials. As with concrete and metal alloys, plastics resulted from people trying to come up with a synthetic substitute for natural materials that were in short supply.

Plastics belong to a group of materials called **polymers.** A polymer is a giant molecule made from the combination of thousands of smaller, "building-block" molecules called **monomers.** American printer and amateur chemist John Wesley Hyatt developed the first plastic material in the 1860s. He made it to replace ivory, which was used to make billiard balls. After many failed experiments, Hyatt combined alcohol and camphor (the

John Wesley Hyatt is best known for discovering a method to simplify the production of plastic celluloid. The major application of the discovery was that, when cut in strips, it could be used as the first photographic film.

material used in mothballs) with guncotton (a material used in place of black powder in firearms) in a large vessel and heated them for several minutes. The result was a thick liquid that could be poured into molds. When the liquid cooled, it became hard. Hyatt had invented celluloid, the first synthetic polymer. As it turns out, celluloid was not used to make billiard balls for very long: Celluloid billiard balls had a nasty habit of exploding when hit the wrong way. Yet, its discovery led to the discovery of other polymers. In **Experiment 13:** *Synthetic Polymer Putty*, you will make a simple polymer using white glue and laundry detergent and discover how a small chemical reaction can result in some very large molecules.

# EXPERIMENT 13

# Synthetic Polymer Putty

## Topic

How is a synthetic polymer produced?

## Introduction

Polymerization is a process in which thousands of small molecules known as monomers join together to form gigantic chains or networks of molecules called polymers. Many man-made compounds—including plastics, synthetic rubber and Styrofoam—are polymers. There are many naturally occurring polymers as well, including the proteins in our bodies and cellulose, which is the main component in wood. In this activity, you will use two common household chemicals to create a simple polymer that has some unusual properties.

## Time Required

45 minutes

## Materials

- box of 20 Mule Team Borax Laundry Detergent (available at most supermarkets)
- bottle of plain white glue (Elmer's works best)
- large metal or plastic mixing bowl
- 2 large (16 oz, 500 mL) disposable plastic cups
- disposable plastic teaspoon
- water
- several paper towels
- goggles or safety glasses

**Safety Note** During this experiment, you will be mixing solutions that could sting if they get into cuts and eyes, so you should wear safety glasses or goggles. If you have sensitive skin, you may also want to wear thin rubber or latex exam gloves. Use caution not to splash the solutions on clothing or furniture. Wipe up any spills immediately with a damp paper towel. It is recommended that you conduct this activity under the supervision of a responsible adult.

## Procedure

1. Put on the safety glasses before conducting this experiment. Fill one of the plastic cups halfway with white glue. Fill the other cup ¾ full of water. Add 4 teaspoons (20 mL) of borax powder to the cup with the water and stir until the powder dissolves. Observe the properties of each liquid. Touch the borax solution with the index finger of your right hand and rub it between that finger and your thumb. Do the same with the glue using the index finger of your left hand, and then compare how the two solutions feel.

2. Pour the white glue into the mixing bowl. Pour the borax solution on top of the glue. Observe what happens to the surface of the glue when the borax

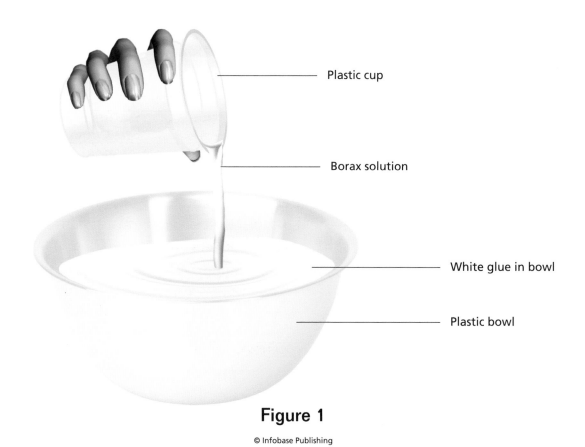

Plastic cup

Borax solution

White glue in bowl

Plastic bowl

**Figure 1**

hits it. Use the plastic spoon to mix the two solutions and observe what happens.

3. After about five minutes, grab a handful of the glue/borax mixture and squeeze it into a ball. Make sure to hold your hand over the bowl so that none of the excess liquid splashes out. Rinse the glue ball under some cold water for about 30 seconds and dry it with a paper towel. Take the glue ball and drop it on a hard surface, such as a table or wooden floor. Observe what the ball does when it hits the hard surface.

## Analysis

1. How did the glue and borax solutions feel when you rubbed them between your fingers?

2. What happened to the surface of the glue when the borax solution hit it?

3. How did the properties of the glue change when it mixed with the borax solution?

4. What did the glue ball do when you dropped it on the hard surface?

## What's Going On?

The material that you formed in this experiment is an example of a cross-linked polymer. White glue, which has the chemical name polyvinyl acetate, is also a polymer consisting of long chains of molecules. This type of polymer is known as a liner addition polymer because the molecules are all in a line. In this form, the polymer chains are free to slide past one another so the glue behaves like a thick, viscous liquid. When the borax solution (chemical name sodium tetraborate) was added to the glue, the chains of molecules began to bond together in a sideways direction, turning the liquid glue into a semisolid material. This process is known as cross-linking. It results in a network polymer, which is much more rigid than a linear polymer. In this particular case, the network polymer you created is elastic, which is why the ball bounces.

## Our Findings

1. The glue was sticky, and the borax solution felt slippery.

2. The glue formed a skin on top.

3. The glue turned thick and began to look like rubber.

4. The glue ball bounced.

## PROPERTIES OF PLASTICS

While John Wesley Hyatt was inventing celluloid, other scientists and inventors were experimenting with a variety of chemicals in an attempt to create other compounds that had useful properties. In 1872, German chemist Adolf von Baeyer used phenol and formaldehyde to make a compound that eventually would be marketed as Bakelite, the first true synthetic plastic. Bakelite is known as a thermosetting plastic because after it is poured into a mold and cooled, it does not change form again when reheated. This is different from thermoplastics, such as vinyl and nylon, which can be repeatedly melted and reshaped many times over. Today, there are hundreds of plastics, many with some unusual properties. In **Experiment 14:** *Unique Properties of Plastics*, you will test several common plastic items to see some of their special properties.

Adolf von Baeyer won the 1905 Nobel Prize for chemistry. He once said, "I have never planned my experiments to find out if I was right, but [instead] to see how the compounds behave."

# Unique Properties of Plastics

## Topic:

What are some of the properties that different plastics display?

## Introduction

Today, we have dozens of specialized plastics that are used to make things. Many things—including rope, fabrics, car bumpers, and baby bottles—are made from plastics. In some cases, such as in the packaging of food and beverages, plastics have all but replaced more traditional materials, such as glass or paper. In this activity, you will test several common plastic products and compare them to their traditional counterparts to see how they stack up.

### Time Required

45 minutes

### Materials

- clean, empty 12-oz (400 mL) plastic beverage bottle
- clean, empty 12-oz (400 mL) glass beverage bottle
- 12-in.-long (30 cm) sheet of clear plastic wrap
- 12-in.-long (30 cm) sheet of aluminum foil
- 50 to 100 pennies
- 24-in.-long (60 cm) piece of plastic fishing line (same thickness as cotton string)
- 24-in.-long (60 cm) piece of thin cotton package string (same thickness as fishing line)
- small ceramic cereal or soup bowl
- scale for weighing small quantities (postal scale, food scale, or three-beam balance)
- work gloves

> **Safety Note** No special safety precautions are needed for this activity. Please review and follow the safety guidelines before proceeding.

## Procedure

1. Pick up the glass bottle in one hand and the plastic bottle in the other. Observe the two bottles closely. Give each bottle a gentle squeeze and then weigh each bottle on the scale. Record the properties of each bottle.

2. Hold the sheet of plastic wrap by the edges and gently stretch it over the top of the ceramic bowl so that it tightly covers the entire top of the bowl. As shown in Figure 1, place pennies on top of the plastic and count how many pennies the plastic will hold until it either rips or slips off the top of the bowl. Record the number of pennies the plastic wrap held. Repeat the procedure using a sheet of aluminum foil stretched over the same bowl. After comparing the two materials with the pennies, crumple both the plastic wrap and the aluminum foil sheets into tight balls and then try to smooth them into flat sheets again. Record your observations.

Plastic wrap stretched-tight over bowl

Pennies on top of plastic wrap

**Figure 1**

© Infobase Publishing

3. Put on the work gloves and tightly grasp one end of the cotton string in each hand. Start pulling on the string, steadily increasing the tension, until the string breaks. Repeat the procedure with the fishing line and compare the amount of force needed to break each of them.

## Analysis

1. Based on your observations, what are some of the advantages to packaging beverages in plastic containers, rather than glass containers?

2. Which type of wrap held the most pennies before either slipping or tearing?

3. Which type of wrap was easier to smooth out after being crumpled?

4. Which type of line required the most force to break it?

### What's Going On?

The use of plastics has steadily increased over the last few decades, in part because plastics can be made to have a variety of unique properties. Beverage bottles made from polyethylene terephthalate (called PET, for short) have all but replaced glass bottles for packaging soft drinks because they are just as strong, far less likely to break, and weigh much less. This not only saves on shipping costs, but also makes them easier for consumers to carry. When it comes to tying things up, rope and twine made from synthetic fibers, such as nylon, are much stronger and less likely to unravel and fray than are their natural-fiber counterparts. For storing leftover food, plastic wrap is superior to aluminum foil because it is able to stretch, making an airtight seal. If it does get crumpled, plastic wrap can be straightened out and used again, while aluminum foil usually will tear.

For all the benefits that plastics offer, they do pose some problems. Most plastic products are made from petroleum, which is a nonrenewable resource. Recent studies have shown that some plastic beverage containers have the potential to leach dangerous chemicals into the drinks that they hold. Perhaps the biggest problem with plastics is that when it comes time to dispose of them, they are still rather difficult to recycle. Because most plastics are only slightly biodegradable, they last a very long time in landfills or as roadside litter.

## Our Findings

1. Beverage bottles made from plastic are flexible, lightweight, and difficult to break.

2. The plastic wrap made a much tighter seal on the bowl.

3. The plastic wrap was much easier to flatten out and use again.

4. The plastic fishing line was much stronger than the cotton string.

## POLYMERS AND PACKAGING

As we saw in the previous experiment, one of the most popular places that plastics are used these days is in packaging. If you look hard enough, you can still find places where you are presented with a choice of packaging materials. One place is the grocery store checkout, where they ask if you would rather have a paper or plastic bag. Both of these man-made materials have been used for carrying groceries for years, but are they equal to all tasks? In **Experiment 15: *Paper vs. Plastic***, you will have the opportunity to do some consumer product testing to see which material is better suited to a variety of jobs.

Many grocery stores have both plastic and paper bags available. While some states and cities are considering passing laws to ban or limit the use of plastic bags, a growing number of grocery stores now sell reusable bags or recycle old plastic bags.

## EXPERIMENT 15  Paper vs. Plastic

### Topic

Which type of material is most effective for carrying different types of groceries?

### Introduction

These days, plastic bags seem to be everywhere. We use them to package our trash, wrap our lunches, and carry our groceries. Since they were first introduced several decades ago, plastic grocery bags have met with mixed reviews. Many people still would rather use the more traditional brown paper bag, and will even complain when stores do not have them available. In this activity, you will compare the behavior of paper and plastic bags to see if either is clearly superior at performing several tasks.

### Time Required

45 minutes for initial experiment, 5 minutes the second day for observations

### Materials

- 2 lab thermometers
- 3 brown paper grocery bags without tears or holes
- 3 plastic grocery bags without tears or holes
- 2 zip-top sandwich bags
- small (3 oz, or 100 mL) bathroom cup
- 10 to 15 cans of soup, vegetables, or similar-sized groceries
- 6 ice cubes
- raw onion

- knife and cutting board

- watch or timer

- large bucket of water

- person to assist you

## Procedure

1. Dry weight loading: Have your assistant open a paper grocery bag and grasp it firmly by the top edges (see Figure 1). Fill the bag with cans of food until the bag begins to rip. Count how many cans the bag held before it tore and record your observations. Repeat the same procedure using the plastic grocery bag held open by the handles.

Cans

**Figure 1**

© Infobase Publishing

2. Wet weight loading: Fill the bathroom cup with water and pour the water into the bottom of a second paper grocery bag. Pour a second cup of water into the bottom of the second plastic grocery bag. Allow the two bags to sit for two minutes and dump out any excess water. Repeat Step 1.

3. Insulating frozen food: Place three ice cubes in each plastic sandwich bag and zip the tops tightly closed. Place one bag of ice in the bottom of the third paper grocery bag and the other in the bottom of the third plastic grocery bag. Place the two lab thermometers side by side on a table or countertop and record the temperature of each. (They should be the same.) Rest the paper bag with the ice on top of one thermometer and the plastic grocery bag with the ice on top of the other. Allow both bags to sit undisturbed for one minute. Remove them from the thermometers and record the temperatures again. The bag that resulted in a higher reading on the thermometer was the better insulator because it kept the cold in the bag.

4. Blocking odors: Carefully use the knife and cutting board to slice the raw onion in half. Place one half into the paper bag that you used in Step 3 and the other half in the plastic bag that you used in Step 3. Close the top of each bag as tightly as possible. Allow the two bags to sit undisturbed for two minutes. Hold the bottom of each bag close to your nose and observe which one has the strongest onion smell. Record your observations.

5. Effect on the environment: Remove the onion from each bag and place both bags side by side in the bucket of water. Make sure they are submerged. Allow them to sit undisturbed for 24 hours. Carefully remove each bag from the water and observe its condition.

## Analysis

1. Which type of bag is best for carrying the most weight of dry groceries?

2. Which type of bag is best for carrying the most weight of damp groceries?

3. Which type of bag would be best for carrying frozen food home from the store if you wanted to keep it from melting?

4. Which type of bag would work best for keeping the smell of raw fish from getting out?

5. Which type of bag would be less harmful for the environment if they both were dumped in a lake or stream?

## What's Going On?

The battle between users of paper and plastic grocery bags has raged almost since plastic bags were introduced. Based on the results of your tests, it would seem that there is no clear-cut winner. Each type of bag has its own advantages and disadvantages. Both types of bag can carry comparable weights when they are dry, but the plastic bag is much stronger when it is wet. The paper bag is a better insulator, so it works better for keeping frozen food cold. Both bags allowed the smell of the onion to come through, but the plastic contained it a little better.

The biggest difference between plastic and paper has to do with the long-term effect on the environment. When paper bags get wet, they begin to fall apart. If a paper bag is out in the environment, or placed in a landfill, it begins to disintegrate or biodegrade. Plastic bags, on the other hand, can last for decades without biodegrading. Plastic grocery bags are often blown off trash heaps by the wind and find their way into natural environments, where they can harm fish and other wildlife. So what's the best choice of grocery bag? Simple, don't use either. Bring a cloth or canvas bag to the store. These bags are much stronger than either plastic or paper. They have better insulating properties and can be washed to remove odors. They can be reused many times. When they finally wear out, they will biodegrade.

## Our Findings

1. Both bags should have been about equal when it came to carrying dry weight.

2. The plastic bag could carry much more weight when it was wet.

3. The paper bag was a better insulator, so it would be better for keeping food items frozen on the trip home from the store.

4. The plastic bag was better at blocking odors.

5. The paper bag would be less harmful for the environment because it breaks down in water.

## FILLING THE GAPS

One of the most important roles that modern polymers play is as sealants and fillers in gaps and spaces, around sinks and bathtubs, and around windows and doorframes. The general term used to describe these products is *caulk*. Early on, one of the most important uses of caulk was in the construction of boats and ships, where it was wedged between the planks of wood used in the hulls. Unless these spaces were properly sealed, a boat would quickly spring leaks and eventually sink.

Today, caulking compounds are important in a home because they reduce the movement of air in and out of a building. This helps to save energy. These compounds also stop water from

A caulking gun is used to caulk a window for insulation purposes.

flowing into unwanted places, such as behind walls and under floors near showers and bathtubs.

The caulking compounds originally used to plug the spaces in building walls were made out of natural materials, such as wadded-up cotton and a substance known as oakum, which was hemp fibers coated with pine tar. These worked fairly well, but they had to be replaced on a regular basis. Later, materials such as plaster and cement were used, but they too were inefficient. They would shrink and crack over time. What people needed were caulking compounds that would stick in the spaces and remain flexible without shrinking. This didn't come about until modern polymers were invented. Today, people involved in the construction industry have dozens of different caulking products to choose from, each with its own special properties. In **Experiment 16**: *Properties of Caulking Compounds*, you are going to test three of the most popular products to see how they compare.

# EXPERIMENT 16

# Properties of Caulking Compounds

## Topic

What are some of the special properties of different caulking compounds?

## Introduction

In building construction, little spaces can often lead to big expenses! Small cracks around windows and doors—or between a building's foundation and a wall—allow moisture, air, and insects to get into a building. This can result in rotting wood and wasted energy. To help solve the problem, homeowners and people in the construction trades turn to a variety of caulking compounds to help seal up the cracks. There are dozens of caulks and sealants available today. Many use high-tech synthetic polymers to get the job done. In this activity, you are going to compare three materials to see how effective they are at sealing cracks. Each one of these compounds has its own unique chemistry and properties.

## Time Required

30 minutes setup time 24 hours drying time, and 10 minutes for testing

## Materials

- 3 large (12-in., or 30-cm) paper plates

- 3 disposable plastic teaspoons

- 3 pieces of ¼-in. (5 mm) wire mesh cut into 6-in. (15-cm) squares (available at most hardware or home improvement stores)

- small tube of 100% silicone sealant (available at most hardware or home improvement stores)

- small tube or container of premixed joint compound (available at most hardware or home improvement stores)

- small tube of latex bathroom caulk (available at most hardware or home improvement stores)
- small jar of water-based paint
- marker
- small paintbrush
- scissors
- rubber gloves

**Safety Note** You should wear rubber gloves when handling the caulking compounds. Be careful not to get any of the compounds on your clothes or furniture. Avoid contact with skin and eyes. It is recommended that you conduct this activity under the supervision of a responsible adult.

## Procedure

1. Use the marker to label the edge of one plate "silicone sealant," the second plate "joint compound," and the final plate "latex caulk." Place one piece of wire mesh on each plate. Use the scissors to snip off the end of each of the caulking tubes.

2. As in Figure 1, squeeze a thick bead of silicone sealant onto the middle of the screen on the plate marked "silicone sealant." Carefully observe

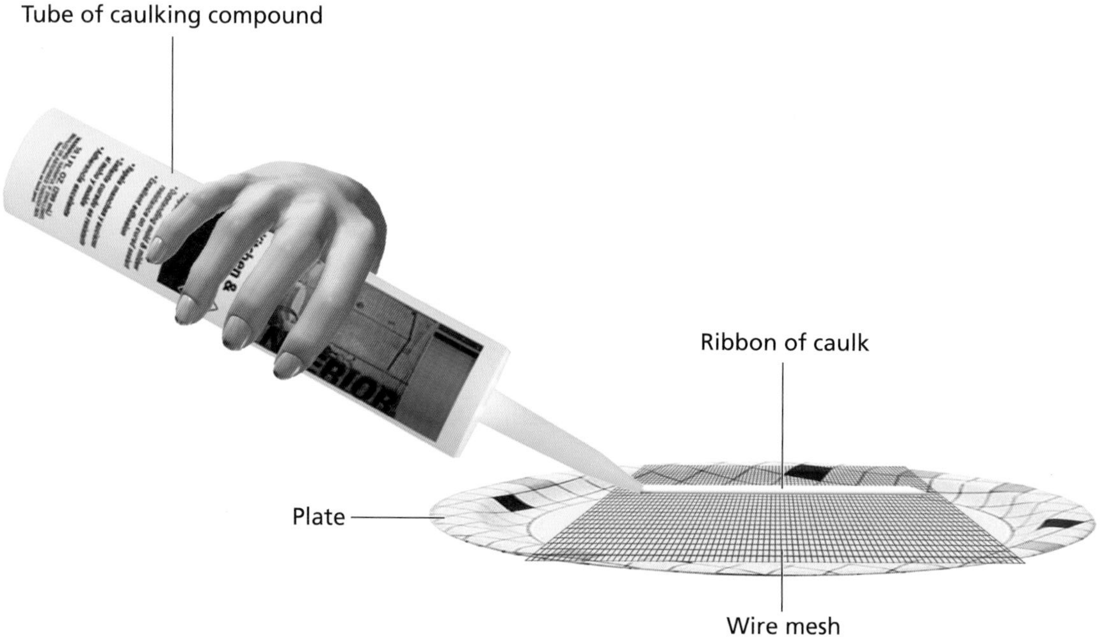

Tube of caulking compound

Ribbon of caulk

Plate

Wire mesh

**Figure 1**

the consistency of the material as it comes out of the tube. Use the back of one of the plastic teaspoons to spread the sealant over the middle of the screen. There should be enough material to cover at least 10 squares with a layer that is about ¼ in. (5 mm) thick. Note the consistency of the material as you spread it across the screen. Record your observations and throw the spoon away.

3. Repeat Step 2 using the joint compound and again using the latex caulk. Use a clean spoon each time. Place the plates where they can sit undisturbed to dry for 24 hours.

4. After the three compounds have dried, touch the top of each screen with your fingers to compare the texture of each material. Use the paint and brush to paint a small section of each compound and observe what happens. Pick up each screen by the edges. While holding a screen over the plate, bend it back and forth several times and observe what happens to the compound on the screen as it flexes.

## Analysis

1. How did the three compounds appear when they first came out of the tubes?

2. What happened when you tried to spread the compounds with the spoons?

3. How did the three compounds feel after they had time to dry?

4. What happened when you tried to paint the three compounds?

5. What happened to the compounds when you bent the screens back and forth?

### What's Going On?

Caulking compounds have come a long way since the days when settlers stuffed mud and straw between logs in their cabins. Over the last half-century, scientists have come up with a variety of specialized caulking compounds designed to work in a variety of conditions and situations. The most basic type of construction filler is joint compound, or "spackling compound." This material is similar to plaster and is most often used to fill cracks in old plaster walls and the spaces between individual sheets of plasterboard (drywall) in new construction. Joint compound dries quickly and can be sanded to a smooth finish. After it has hardened, it is easy to paint. Yet, joint compound cracks under stress, meaning that it may fall out of the space that it's filling.

Latex caulk is ideal for filling in large spaces around bathtubs, sinks, and showers. It can be squeezed into oddly shaped spaces, and it adheres well to ceramic tiles and porcelain. When latex caulk is wet, it can be smoothed with a wet finger or sponge. When it dries, it can be sanded and painted. As latex caulk dries, it tends to shrink a little. Over time, it becomes brittle and cracks. Another major drawback is that it does not adhere to metals.

Silicone sealant is the most versatile (and expensive) of the types of caulking compound you tested. It adheres to almost any type of material and stays flexible after it dries. Silicone does not shrink, and it can be stretched or compressed without cracking. Silicone sealant will stick to metals and painted surfaces, but surprisingly, paint will not stick to it.

## Our Findings

1. The silicone was a sticky thin gel, the latex caulk was a thick gel, and the joint compound was a paste.
2. The silicone was easy to spread, but it stuck to the spoon. The latex was difficult to spread but did not stick to the spoon. The joint compound spread smoothly.
3. The silicone felt rubbery. The latex was stiff but flexible. The joint compound was hard.
4. The paint covered the latex caulk and joint compound, but it would not stick to the silicone.
5. The silicone stayed in the screen and flexed. The latex fell out. The joint compound cracked and fell apart.

## PAINTING WITH POLYMERS

Another important role that polymers have played is in the development of modern paints. Paints are liquids that are applied to the surface of an object to change its color or design. The first known use of paints dates back to about 20,000 years ago, when ancient artists used natural pigments to create cave paintings that showed hunting scenes. In addition to their artistic value, paints are important because they help protect surfaces from the effects of weather. Earlier, we discussed how steel bridges are painted to keep the metal from corroding. In a similar fashion, wooden objects are painted to keep the wood from rotting. In **Experiment 17:** *Latex vs. Oil-based Paint,* you are going to test two types of modern paint to see how they compare with each other.

# Latex vs. Oil-based Paint

## Topic

What are some of the advantages and disadvantages of latex and oil-based paint?

## Introduction

In order to work well, paint needs three main components; a pigment to provide the color, a binder that makes it stick to a surface, and a solvent that keeps it liquid. Once exposed to the air, the solvent begins to evaporate and dry, forming a solid layer on the outer surface of an object. The earliest paints were made from plants or mineral pigments, including iron oxide, a type of rust. The pigment was then mixed with substances such as animal fat, natural glue from plants and fish, and even blood. In the 1700s, people discovered that linseed oil would serve as an even better binder, and oil-based paints became the standard for many years. Oil paints are still used in many applications, but as synthetic polymers became better understood, they became incorporated as binders. The first latex paints were marketed in the late 1940s. Today, they are the most popular type used by homeowners. In this activity, you are going to compare modern latex paint with a more traditional oil-based paint to rate the advantages of each.

## Time Required

20 minutes preparation, 2 hours to observe reaction, 48-hour drying time, and 5 minutes observation on each day

## Materials

- small can of latex paint
- small can of oil paint
- 2 small disposable paintbrushes
- 2 sheets of aluminum foil, each about 12 in. (30 cm) long

- 2 sticks for stirring paint

- paper towels

- marker

- masking tape

- container of mineral spirits

- 2 large (16 oz, or 500 mL) disposable plastic cups of water

- a well-ventilated room

- screwdriver for opening paint can

- newspapers

- adult to assist you

**Safety Note** This activity should be conducted in a well-ventilated area. Oil-based paint is flammable; do not use it near an open flame or heat source. Do not get paint on your clothes or furniture and avoid contact with skin and eyes. If you do spill any of the oil-based paint, you must use a paper towel soaked in mineral spirits to clean it up immediately. It is recommended that you conduct this activity under the supervision of a responsible adult.

## Procedure

1. Spread out the newspapers on the floor or table. Place the paint cans on top of the newspapers and remove their lids. Look at the paint inside each can. Gently stir each can, being careful not to spill any paint. Observe the way each type of paint mixes and note any odor. After the paints are mixed, remove the stirring sticks and allow them to drip into the cans. Then wrap them in paper towels and place them off to the side.

2. Place the two sheets of aluminum foil on the newspaper, dull side up. Use a piece of masking tape to label one foil "latex paint" and the other "oil-based paint."

3. Dip one paintbrush into the oil-based paint and paint a square on the foil labeled "oil-based paint." The square should be about 6 in. (15 cm) on a side. Make certain that the paint is smooth and even. When you are finished, place the brush in one of the cups of water. Repeat the procedure with the other brush, using the latex paint and the second piece of foil. Place both pieces of foil in a safe location to dry for two hours.

**Figure 1**

© Infobase Publishing

4. Observe the two paintbrushes in the cups of water. Swish each around a few times and watch what happens to the water and paint. Remove each paintbrush and wrap its wet end in a paper towel before discarding.

5. After two hours have passed, return to the foil and test each paint spot with your finger. Do this again after 24 hours and 48 hours. After two days have passed, pick up each piece of foil by the edges, crumple it a few times, and then spread it out again. Observe what happens to the paint spot on each piece of foil. When finished, crumple the foil into a ball (with the painted side on the inside) and discard in the trash. Do not recycle it.

## Analysis

1. How did the two paints appear before mixing?
2. How did the two paints smell?
3. How well did each type of paint cover the foil?
4. What happened to the two paintbrushes when you placed them in the water?
5. How long did it take for each type of paint to dry?
6. What happened to the two paint spots when you crumpled the foil?

## What's Going On?

Latex and oil-based paint are equally effective at covering many types of surfaces. They are both durable and wear well. Where they differ is in how convenient they are to use. Latex paints use water as the solvent and a polymer such as polyvinyl acetate as the binder. This means that these paints can be easily cleaned with soap and water when they are still wet. They emit only a slight odor. Because water evaporates quickly, latex paints also dry fast, usually in a few hours. As you just discovered, oil-based paints behave differently.

Chemically speaking, water and oil are opposites. Water is a polar molecule. This means that the two ends of the molecule behave like electrically charged particles with opposite charges. Oil is a nonpolar molecule. As a result, oil and water don't mix. Because of this, oil-based paints must use a solvent other than water. In most cases, the solvent is a substance known as turpentine, which is a complex hydrocarbon made from the sap found in pine trees. Turpentine has a noxious odor, so until an oil-based paint dries (which may take up to several days), it is quite smelly. Turpentine also is highly flammable. Finally, when it comes time to clean brushes and spills of oil-based paint, only a hydrocarbon-based solvent, such as turpentine or mineral spirits, can be used.

Why do people still use oil-based paints if latex paints can do the same job and are far more convenient? Part of the answer lies in tradition. Oil-based paints have been used for centuries, and old habits die hard. Also, latex paints are not suited for every application. When water-based paints are used on iron or steel, they tend to rust.

## Our Findings

1. The oil-based paint most likely had a layer of oil floating at the top of the can, while the latex paint may have had only a little separation.

2. The oil-based paint had a distinctive harsh petroleum smell, while the latex paint had only a faint odor.

3. Both paints covered the foil quite well, leaving a smooth texture.

4. The brush with the latex paint began to quickly mix with the water, while the water simply beaded up on the surface of the oil-based paintbrush.

5. The latex paint dried in about two hours. The oil-based paint may have stayed "tacky" to the touch for up to two days.

6. The dry paint adhered equally well to both pieces of foil even when it was crumpled.

## A PROBLEM WITH PLASTICS

The development of new types of synthetic polymers has exploded during the last half century. There is hardly a place in our modern world where plastics have not come into play. As the use of synthetic polymers gained acceptance in different businesses and industries, people became aware of a growing problem; plastics also were showing up in many places where we did not want them. The media was filled with images of seabirds and mammals being choked by plastic six-pack holders that wound up in the ocean, and plastic grocery bags stuck high in trees or wrapped around lampposts. Plastic beverage bottles littered the highways, and appliances with plastic cases were piling up in landfills. It turned out that one of the biggest advantages of plastics also was a liability: plastics last a long time.

When paper and metal alloys are exposed to water, air, and soil microbes, they tend to disintegrate and return to their component atoms and molecules. Scientists call these types of materials biodegradable. Plastics usually are not biodegradable. Left in the environment, a plastic soda bottle or CD cover can last hundreds of years. So what can we do once a plastic product has reached the end of its useful life? One answer is to recycle it. In **Experiment 18:** *Plastics Can Be Recycled,* we will examine what steps have to be taken in order for plastics to be recycled.

# EXPERIMENT 18

# Plastics Can Be Recycled

## Topic

Some plastic have properties that allow them to be recycled.

## Introduction

Plastics are a group of synthetic polymers that have many uses in our modern world. Like metals, plastics have a wide range of properties, and each type of plastic has its own chemical formula. For much of the last century, when metal products reached the end of their usefulness, they were recycled. In theory, plastics can be recycled, too.

Recycling is a process where waste material is separated, cleaned of contaminants, and eventually turned back into new products. Recycling not only reduces waste, but also saves energy and resources. Recycled materials replace raw materials that would normally be extracted from the ground. Because of their high value, metals such as copper, brass, aluminum, and lead have been recycled for most of the last century. In recent decades, the recycling of paper and glass also has become common, but plastic recycling is still a relatively new process. One challenge to widespread plastic recycling is the fact that there are many different types of plastic. Just as aluminum scrap must be sorted from copper before recycling, different types of plastic must be separated from one another. To make the separation of plastics easier, manufactures now use a special recycling code on most items. In this activity, you are going to use this code to learn about the properties of each type of plastic.

### Time Required

50 minutes of setup time

### Materials

- assortment of clean, empty plastic containers, including items such as a soda bottle, milk bottle, detergent bottle, ketchup bottle, mayonnaise jar, yogurt container, CD case, sandwich bag, egg carton, plastic pipe

- acetone (nail polish remover)
- cotton swab
- water
- small (1 quart, or 1,000 mL) metal or glass saucepan
- salt
- tablespoon
- measuring cup
- tongs or large tweezers
- hot plate or stove
- strong scissors
- safety goggles
- adult to assist you

**Safety Note** Review and follow the safety guidelines. Take special care when using the hot plate or stove. Acetone is highly flammable. KEEP IT AWAY FROM THE HOT PLATE OR STOVE. Use it in a well-ventilated area and do not let it drip on clothing or furniture. If it should get on your skin, wash it immediately. Wear goggles or safety glasses when cutting the plastics and testing with acetone. This activity should be conducted under the supervision of a responsible adult.

## Procedure

1. Lay out the pieces of plastic and observe each carefully. Look for the recycling code symbol on each. In the case of the plastic bags, the code will be on the box in which they came. A chart showing the code is given in Figure 1, along with the symbol.

2. If possible, select six pieces of plastic that each have a different code. Write the name of the object and the code in the first column of the data table.

3. Fold each piece of plastic and see if it bends or breaks. Record your results on the data table.

4. Test each piece of plastic to see if it can be stretched. Record your findings on the data table.

**Recycling Codes**

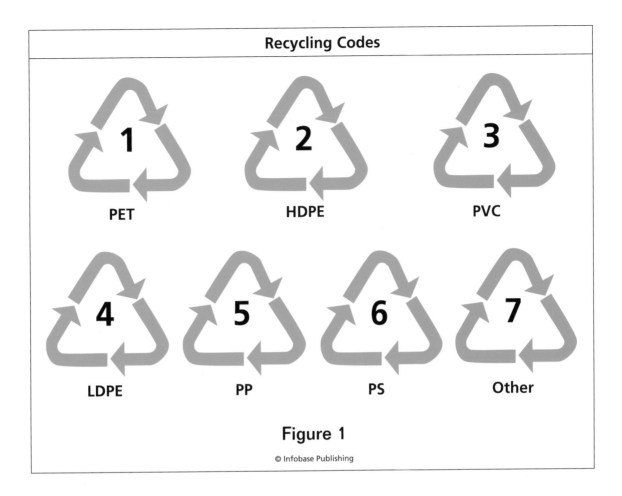

PET      HDPE      PVC

LDPE    PP    PS    Other

**Figure 1**

5. Use the scissors to cut each sample into small pieces, each about 1 in. (2.5 cm) square. Fill the sauce pan with 1 cup (250 mL) of water. Test each square of plastic to see if it floats or sinks. Record your results on the data table.

6. Add 5 tablespoons (75 mL) of salt to the water and stir until it dissolves. Test each plastic square again to see if it sinks or floats. Record your results on the data table.

7. Empty the water from the pan and rinse it well. Fill the pan with 1 cup (250 mL) of fresh water and heat it on the stove or hot plate until it begins to boil. Drop each plastic square in the water and then turn off the heat. Allow the plastic pieces to sit in the hot water for five minutes and then remove each with the tongs or tweezers. Try bending the plastic again to see if the heating had any effect on its flexibility and record your results on the data table.

8. Carefully dip the cotton swab in the acetone and rub it on each piece of plastic. Examine the plastic to see if the acetone had any effect. Record your results in the data table.

| Type of Plastic/ Recycling Codes | Breaks or Bends | Will or Will Not Stretch | Floats in Water | Floats in Salt Water | Softens in Hot Water | Reacts with Acetone | Descriptive Summary Statement |
|---|---|---|---|---|---|---|---|
| | | | | | | | |
| | | | | | | | |
| | | | | | | | |
| | | | | | | | |
| | | | | | | | |
| | | | | | | | |

Data Table 1

## Analysis

1. What is the recycling code on the most flexible types of plastic?
2. What is the recycling code for the plastic that floated in water? In salt water?
3. From your analysis of the plastic samples, what is the code on the plastic that would make the best shampoo bottle (flexible, but will not break)? What is the code on the type that would make the best coffee cup (strong, resistant to heat, does not break easily)?

## What's Going On?

Different types of plastic have different properties and characteristics. Plastics that are easy to bend and soften in hot water are easiest to recycle. They can be melted down and made into new forms or entirely new items. Soft-drink bottles and lightweight food containers are made from polyethylene terephthalate (PET). This is the most commonly recycled type of plastic. It often is turned into fibers to be used in carpets or as fiberfill insulation in garments. Milk, juice, and detergent containers have a different chemistry and properties. They are made from high-density polyethylene (HDPE). These are turned into plastic pipes and plastic lumber. Shampoo bottles and clear food-storage containers usually are made from polyvinyl chloride (PVC). Plastic storage bags are made from low-density polyethylene (LDPE). Polypropylene (PP) is used to make strong containers, such as ketchup bottles and medicine bottles. Polystyrene (PS) is used in hard plastics, such as CD cases and plastic cutlery.

## Our Findings

1. The recycling code on most flexible plastics is LDPE.
2. The recycling code for the plastic that floated in water and salt water is PET.
3. The best shampoo bottle code would be PVC. The best coffee cup would be PS.

## THE POWER AND POTENTIAL OF POLYMERS

Since they were first introduced about 150 years ago, synthetic polymers in general (and plastics, specifically) have made a major impact on society. In the early years, plastics were a curiosity. Items made from plastic were considered cheap and of lesser value than those made of traditional materials. As time went on, manufacturers became more aware of the versatility of plastics and incorporated them into many more products.

Today, it's hard to imagine a world without synthetic polymers, and the list of uses for them is still growing. Chemists continue to make discoveries in polymer research that will continue to change the way we live. Of all the man-made materials developed in the history of our planet, synthetic polymers have had the greatest impact on human society. Though plastics have been beneficial, they have caused many environmental problems. As with all man-made materials, care must be taken to use them wisely to minimize their long-term impact on the environment.

# Keep It Clean

et's face it: We live in a dirty world. Grease, grime, soil, and soot are all around us. They get on our hands and faces, in our clothes, and on furniture and fabrics. For thousands of years, people have found ways to get things clean. The manufacturing and sale of cleaning agents—for everything from countertops and clothing to cars and cabinets—is a huge industry.

In the early days, people weren't all that concerned with getting things clean. If they needed to clean something, they would rinse it in running water. Beating clothes against a stone in a stream usually got them clean. The first cleaning agents probably were discovered by accident. People found that certain plants, such as soapworts and soapberries, contained a substance that helped remove grease and grime. Then, about 4,000 years ago, the Babylonians (who lived in the area that is now Iraq) went out of their way to make the first cleaning agents.

The Babylonians discovered that soaking wood and plant ashes in water would make a liquid solution that could help clean clothes and other items. Although they didn't know it at the time, they were using something called the carbonate ion. This is an alkali chemical found in most soaps. Later, in about 600 B.C., the Phoenicians (who lived in the area that is now coastal Lebanon, Syria, and Israel) mixed goat tallow with ashes to make the first soaplike substance. From then on, most soap formulas included a fat and an alkali chemical. Because of a shortage of animal fat used in making soap during World War I, the Germans pioneered the first wide-scale development of synthetic detergents. Today, people have a range of soaps and detergents from which to choose. All have one thing in common: They are designed to make water more effective at cutting grease. In **Experiment 19:** *Cleaning Properties of Detergents,* you will test a modern detergent and see why water alone won't do the trick when it comes to getting things clean.

# EXPERIMENT 19
# Cleaning Properties of Detergents

## Topic

Why must soap and detergent be added to water to make it an effective cleaner?

## Introduction

If you have ever gotten a stain on your clothes or some greasy substance on your hands, you probably have discovered that you need more than plain water to get clean. You usually have to add another substance, such as soap or detergent. A big part of the reason that water alone won't get everything clean is that a water molecule has some interesting chemical properties.

Most people know that the chemical formula for water is $H_2O$. A single water molecule is made of two hydrogen atoms and one oxygen atom. It's shaped a little like Mickey Mouse's head. The two hydrogen atoms are small; they sit next to each other on top of a much larger oxygen atom. (You can think of the hydrogen atoms as Mickey's ears and the oxygen atom as his face.) The water molecule is polar molecule: It has electrically charged ends. The hydrogen end has a positive charge, and the oxygen end has a negative charge.

Most common forms of oil, grease, and grime are made of molecules that are nonpolar. As a result, they will not mix with water. In this experiment, you will

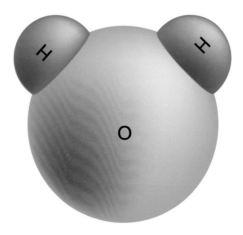

**Figure 1**

discover how soap and detergent can help "bridge the gap" between water and oil and, in the process, help make water a "wetter" substance.

## Time Required

30 minutes

## Materials

- small, clear glass jar (from mayonnaise, baby food, pickles, etc.) with lid, labels, and contents removed
- dishwashing liquid
- medicine dropper
- small cup
- teaspoon
- clean, shiny penny
- water
- cooking oil
- watch or timer
- paper towels

**Safety Note** No special safety precautions are needed for this activity. Please review and follow the safety guidelines before proceeding.

## Procedure

1. Place the penny on top of a paper towel. Dip the medicine dropper into a cup of clean water and squeeze the rubber bulb. Release the bulb; the dropper should fill with water. Hold the end of the dropper above the penny and gently squeeze one drop on top of the penny. (See Figure 2.) Continue placing drops of water on top of the penny and count how many drops of water you can get to rest on the surface of the penny without any spilling over the edge. Carefully observe the shape of the water on top of the penny as the number of drops increases. After the water spills off the

edge of the penny, record the number of drops that you got on the penny and use the paper towel to dry the penny.

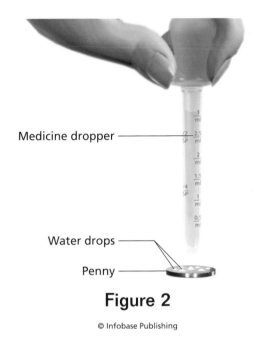

Medicine dropper

Water drops

Penny

**Figure 2**

© Infobase Publishing

2.  Squirt a small amount of dishwashing liquid into the cup of water. Use the teaspoon to mix the detergent with the water, but try not to make too many bubbles. Empty the dropper of water and then repeat Step 1 using the soapy water. Record your observations and the number of water drops the penny was able to hold this time.

3.  Fill the jar about ¹⁄₃ full of clean tap water and ¹⁄₃ full of cooking oil. Make certain to leave some space in the jar. Screw on the lid and observe the two liquids. Shake the jar for about 15 seconds and then observe the liquids again. Allow the jar to stand undisturbed for about a minute and observe the liquids again. Record your observations.

4.  Open the jar and add about 2 teaspoons (10 mL) of dishwashing liquid to the oil and water. Screw the cap on tight again and repeat Step 3. Observe the oil and water mixture after you stop shaking it and compare it with the way it looked at the end of Step 3.

## Analysis

1.  What happened to the water on top of the penny as you continued to add drops in Step 1? What shape did the water make before it finally spilled?

2.  What happened to the water on top of the penny when you added drops of soapy water? How did the number of drops on the penny compare with the number in Step 1?

3.  What happened to the oil and water mixture when you shook it in Step 3?

4. What happened to the oil and water mixture in Step 3 after you allowed it to sit for a minute?

5. What happened to the oil, water, and soap mixture in Step 4 after you shook the bottle and allowed it to stand for a minute?

## What's Going On?

Oil and water don't mix. As a result, washing dishes or clothes with water alone does a very poor job of removing grease. Soap and detergents work as cleaning agents because their molecules have two distinct ends. One side is "hydrophilic," or water loving. This end is attracted to water molecules and can easily bond with them. The other end of the soap molecule is "hydrophobic"—it repels water. This end is attracted to oil molecules. As a result, the soap molecules act as a bridge between the nonpolar oil molecules and the polar water molecules. As the soapy water flows over the material that is being cleaned, it lifts off the grease and dirt and washes it away.

When it comes to cleaning clothes and other fabrics, soap and detergent serve one other important role. They allow water molecules to penetrate the spaces in the tightly woven fabric. As you discovered when you piled the drops of water on top of the penny, water molecules tend to stick together. This force of attraction is called cohesion. Cohesion is why water drops and soap bubbles always have a circular appearance. Right before the water drop burst on top of the penny in Step 1, it almost appeared that the drop had an invisible skin over the top holding it together. This "skin" is called surface tension; it is created by the attraction between the water molecules. Adding soap or detergent to water lessens the attraction between water molecules and breaks the surface tension. This allows the soapy water to penetrate fabrics and get at the dirt, making clothes cleaner.

## Our Findings

1. The water began to pile up on top of the penny until there was one large drop in the shape of a dome or bubble.

2. The water quickly spilled off the top of the penny and never formed the dome shape. You should have been able to get many more drops of water on top of the penny with the plain water than with the soapy water.

3. The oil and water mixed together when they were shaken.

4. After standing for a minute, the oil and water in the jar separated again.

5. After the detergent was added to the oil and water, the two stayed mixed in the jar for a much longer time.

## ACIDS AND BASES AT HOME

Two of the most common chemicals found in both the home and lab are classified as acids and bases. An acid is a substance that usually tastes sour and can dissolve metals. Bases taste bitter and feel slippery on the skin. Both of these substances are highly corrosive at high concentrations. They also can burn skin. Though acids and bases can be dangerous, they also are useful. Orange juice and lemonade are acids; so are tea and coffee. When your stomach is upset, you can drink a base—such as milk of magnesia—to help settle things down.

Acids and bases are chemical opposites of each other, and tend to react with different materials. Rather than guessing whether a substance is an acid or a base, chemists in a lab use a third type of chemical called an indicator. The indicator changes to one color when mixed with an acid, and to another color when mixed with a base. In **Experiment 20:** *The Chemistry of Cleaners,* you will make a simple indicator solution using the juice from a red cabbage and test a variety of common cleaning products to find out if they are acids or bases.

Litmus paper is used to determine to pH of an aqueous solution. The paper has been pretreated with a specific indicator—a mixture of natural dyes that will turn red in response to acidic conditions, blue under alkaline conditions, and purple if the pH is neutral.

# The Chemistry of Cleaners

## Topic

What type of chemicals are most household cleaners?

## Introduction

Many of the substances that we encounter in our homes can be classified as acids or bases. The strength of acids and bases are measured on the pH scale. This name comes from the French term *pouvoir hydrogene*, which means "power of hydrogen." It is a measure of how many hydrogen ions are present in a chemical solution. The pH scale ranges from 0 to 14. When a substance has a pH of 7, it is said to be neutral. From 7 down to a pH of 0, the substance becomes increasingly more acidic. From 7 up to a pH of 14, it becomes increasingly more basic (or alkaline).

Blender

Cabbage juice

Strainer

Plastic cup

**Figure 1**

Modern chemists use a variety of meters to measure the exact pH of solutions, but in the past, the measurement was done using a type of chemical called an indicator. Indicators change colors in the presence of hydrogen ions. One common indicator is called litmus. When it is neutral, litmus is purple. When it encounters an acid, litmus turns red. When it encounters a base, it turns blue. In this activity, you are going to test the pH of different cleaning products to see if they are acids or bases. You will use juice from a red cabbage as an indicator.

## Time Required:

40 minutes

## Materials:

- small head of red cabbage (must be fresh, not bottled)
- electric blender
- metal strainer
- 5 small (8 oz, or 250 mL) clear plastic disposable cups
- large (16 oz, or 500 mL) disposable plastic cup
- water
- paper towels
- 5 plastic teaspoons
- bottle of ammonia
- bottle of white vinegar
- box of baking soda
- dishwashing liquid
- bottle of bleach
- masking tape
- marker
- well-ventilated room

- goggles or safety glasses
- adult to assist you

**Safety Note** This activity should be conducted in a well-ventilated area. Be careful not to get any of the cleaning products on your clothing or furniture. Avoid contact with skin and eyes. Wear safety glasses or goggles when pouring and mixing the chemicals in the indicator solution. If you do spill, use a damp paper towel to clean up the spill immediately. It is recommended that you conduct this activity under the supervision of a responsible adult.

## Procedure

1. Fill the blender ¾ full of cold water. Tear off four or five leaves from the red cabbage and place them in the blender. Put the top on the blender and turn it on the highest speed for about 30 seconds, or until all of the cabbage leaves are chopped into a fine pulp. The water should become dark purple.

2. Carefully remove the top section of the blender and pour the cabbage juice through the strainer into the large plastic cup. Fill the cup about ½ full of juice and replace the blender. Add water to the cup to dilute the cabbage mixture further and then fill each of the smaller cups about ½ full with the diluted mixture. The juice in the test cups should be light purple.

3. Pour a small amount of vinegar into the first cup and stir with a spoon. Vinegar is a type of acid called acetic acid. Record the color of the solution on the data table. In the second cup, add 2 teaspoons (10 mL) of baking soda and stir. Baking soda also is called sodium bicarbonate; it is a base. Record the color on the data table. You now know the acid and base colors for cabbage juice.

4. Take the third cup and add a small amount of ammonia. Use a clean spoon to stir the mixture and observe the color change of the cabbage juice. Repeat the procedure with the dishwashing liquid and bleach in the final two cups. Make certain that you use a clean spoon to stir each solution so that there is no contamination. Record your observations.

| Data Table 1 | |
|---|---|
| **Solution Name** | **Color Change** |
| Vinegar | |
| Baking soda | |
| Dishwashing liquid | |
| Ammonia | |
| Bleach | |

## Analysis

1. What color did the vinegar (acid) turn the cabbage juice?
2. What color did the baking soda (base) turn the cabbage juice?
3. Based on your experiment, what type of substance are the other cleaning products?
4. What color would you expect liquid hand soap to turn cabbage juice?

## What's Going On?

As you discovered in this activity, most of the common cleaning agents are bases. Bases feel slippery when you touch them, and they taste bitter. (Anyone who has ever gotten soap in his or her mouth will know that.) Bases tend to be caustic, which means that if you get a strong one on your skin, it starts to dissolve the skin and fat tissue. That's why bases make good grease cutters and detergents.

## Our Findings

1. The vinegar turned the cabbage juice reddish pink.
2. The baking soda turned it blue-green.
3. All of the other cleaners turned the cabbage juice either blue or green, so they are all bases.
4. Soap should turn the cabbage juice blue-green because it is a base.

## SOFT SOAP AND HARD WATER

Even though soap can be a great cleaning agent, it does have some disadvantages. When soap is used in water that is naturally acidic, the soap itself breaks down and creates free-floating fatty acids in the water. At this point, the soap loses its ability to get things clean. In addition, the free-floating fatty acids start to clump together, forming a wonderfully gross substance called soap scum.

Having water that is naturally acidic is not that common, but the water used for cooking and cleaning in many locations is naturally hard. This does not mean that the water is solid. Water is very good at dissolving substances, such as salt and a variety of other natural minerals. This is especially true of groundwater, which flows naturally under the ground. People who get their water from wells use groundwater as their main source of water. In some locations, water has so many dissolved minerals in it that it is called hard water. Hard water usually contains high levels of calcium, magnesium, and iron. When soap is used in hard water, it reacts to form greasy curds that stick to the side of a sink or bathtub. If you have ever left a "ring around the tub" after taking a bath, it might not be your fault. It could be the type of water that you have.

## DETERGENTS TO THE RESCUE

To solve the problems that soap creates with hard water, many people use water softeners when they do their laundry. Water softeners are chemicals that react with the dissolved minerals in hard water and keep them from reacting with the soap. One of the most common water softening agents is sodium carbonate, which is sold in stores as washing soda.

Early in the 1900s, chemists came up with another way of tackling the hard water problem: They got rid of the soap! The fatty acids and alkaline chemicals in soap can attach to water on one end and grease on the other. Working in labs, scientists created synthetic molecules that had the same attractive properties as soap molecules, without the fatty acids. That meant the end of soap scum and ring around the tub.

These days, the use of synthetic detergents far exceeds the use of soap. We use detergents for washing dishes, cleaning cars, and doing laundry. All you need to do is take a short trip down the "laundry" aisle in any supermarket, and you'll find dozens of detergents, each claiming to be the best. Many include added whiteners. A whitener often is some type of bleach. Bleaching agents have been around since the late 1700s, but chemists have discovered new and improved formulas to whiten clothes and other materials. In **Experiment 21:** *Bleaching Agents*, you will test several common bleaching agents to see how well they work at making things white.

# EXPERIMENT 21

# Bleaching Agents

## Topic

What are some common bleaching agents and how well do they work?

## Introduction

Bleaching agents are man-made chemicals used at home and in industry to remove colors and stains from yarn, fabrics, paper, and other substances. Before there were chemical bleaching agents, the only effective way to whiten materials was to allow them to sit in bright sunlight. This process took days or weeks and, in many cases, some of the underlying colors still remained. In 1774, Swedish chemist Karl Wilhelm Scheele discovered the element chlorine. Then, in 1785, French chemist Claude Berthollet demonstrated that chlorine could be used to remove color from fabrics. This led to the development of bleaching powder, the first man-made bleaching agent, by the Scottish chemist Charles Tennant in 1799. Today, there are dozens of bleaching agents available. In this activity, you are going to test several of them to see which is the most effective at whitening a piece of colored paper.

## Time Required

30 minutes

## Materials

- 4 small (3 oz, or 100 mL) disposable plastic cups
- 4 cotton swabs
- piece of colored construction or copier paper
- bottle of hydrogen peroxide
- bottle of chlorine bleach (Clorox or similar brand)
- bottle of color-safe bleach (Vivid or similar brand)

- water

- scissors

- aluminum foil

- watch or timer

- paper towel

- pen or marker

- counter or table next to a sink

- goggles or safety glasses

- adult to assist you

**Safety Note** This activity should be conducted in a well-ventilated area. Be careful not to get any of the bleaching agents on your clothes or furniture and avoid contact with bare skin and eyes. Wear safety glasses or goggles when conducting this experiment. If you do spill any of the products, use a damp paper towel to clean the spill immediately. When you are finished with the experiment, dump each of the bleaching agents into a sink drain with running water. Rinse the cups with water before throwing them in the trash. It is recommended that you conduct this activity under the supervision of a responsible adult.

## Procedure

1. Tear off a piece of aluminum foil large enough to cover the tabletop or counter next to the sink on which you will be working. The foil will protect the counter from getting stained by any of the bleaching agents. Use the scissors to cut the colored paper into four quarters. Label three of the pieces with the names of the three bleaching agents. Label the fourth piece "water." Do the same for the four plastic cups.

2. As in Figure 1, lay the four pieces of paper next to each other on the foil and place the corresponding cup above each piece. Put on the safety glasses and carefully pour a small amount of each liquid into the proper cup. If any of the liquids spill, clean them up immediately with a damp paper towel. Observe each of the liquids. Wave your hand over the top of each cup to see if any of the liquids have an odor. Do not directly smell the liquid in the cups. Record your observations on your data table.

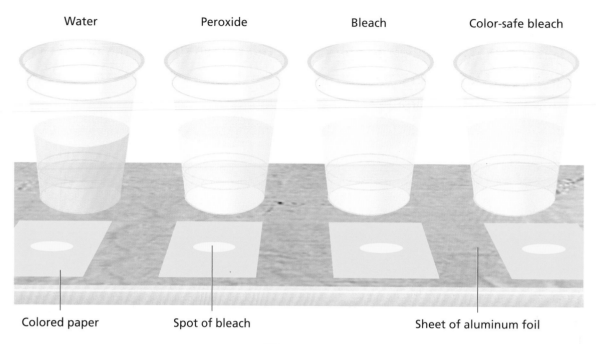

Water          Peroxide          Bleach          Color-safe bleach

Colored paper          Spot of bleach          Sheet of aluminum foil

**Figure 1**

© Infobase Publishing

3. Place a clean cotton swab in each cup. Use the cotton swabs to dab a small amount of liquid in the middle of each piece of paper, making a dot the size of a quarter. Observe what happens to the papers when they get wet. Wait for 10 minutes and observe what the papers look like. Record your results on the data table.

| Data Table 1 | | | | |
|---|---|---|---|---|
| | **Water** | **Bleach** | **Color-safe Bleach** | **Peroxide** |
| Color of liquid | | | | |
| Odor | | | | |
| Immediate effect on paper | | | | |
| Effect on paper after 10 minutes | | | | |

## Analysis

1. How did the four liquids compare when you poured them in the cups?
2. Which liquids had an odor?
3. How did the paper first react when the liquids were applied?
4. How did the papers look after 10 minutes?

### What's Going On?

Bleaching agents work by a chemical process known as oxidation. Oxidation is the same process that happens when a piece of iron rusts or when a piece of wood burns. Bleaching agents are chemicals that release oxygen. When dyes combine with the oxygen, they react chemically and begin to lose their color. The most common and effective bleaching agent is chlorine bleach, which is made of sodium hypochlorite (chemical formula $NaOCl$) and water. Even a small amount of chlorine bleach will quickly remove the color from most clothes. Another effective bleaching agent is hydrogen peroxide solution (chemical formula $H_2O_2$), which is also used as an antiseptic for cleaning wounds. Peroxide also removes pigment from hair, turning it platinum blond. During your experiment, you should have found that color-safe bleach had very little effect on the color of the paper. As the name suggests, color-safe bleaches are chemical compounds that are designed to help remove stains, but to leave the colors of clothes intact. Many color-safe bleaches use a chemical reaction that releases hydrogen peroxide in the water. This oxidizes the stain but leaves the dye in place.

### Our Findings

1. They should all have been colorless.
2. The water had no odor. The peroxide and color-safe bleach had mild odors, while the bleach had a strong odor of chlorine.
3. The bleach immediately started reacting with the paper. The other three simply got wet.
4. After standing for 10 minutes, the spot made with bleach turned bright white. The spot made with the peroxide was lighter in color, but the color was still present. The spot made with the color-safe bleach only changed color slightly. The spot with the water showed no change in color.

## DANGEROUS CHEMICALS IN THE HOME

By now, you've probably realized that even though your house may not look like a chemistry lab, it is full of potentially dangerous chemicals. Substances that are used for bleaching fabrics, unclogging drains, cleaning ovens, polishing furniture, and shining glass contain many of the same chemical compounds found in an industrial lab. Some, such as chlorine bleach, have toxic fumes, and most are poisonous and potentially deadly if swallowed. Even though they are used in homes every day, few people actually take the time to read the warning labels or know just how dangerous some of these substances really are. If you or any of your family members are using these substances, make certain that you follow the directions on the container and know what to do in case of an accidental spill. Safe science is something that we all need to practice, whether it is in a lab or in the kitchen.

# 5

# Things for the Body

So far, we've covered a range of man-made materials. Some, such as concrete and metal alloys, are used in the construction of bridges and buildings. Others, such as insulation and paint, protect other materials from the forces of nature. We've seen how polymers can be used for just about everything and how cleaning agents help keep our clothes and possessions bright. In this chapter, we're going to concentrate on two of the most important categories of man-made materials: cosmetics and drugs. The first may make your life more exciting; the second, you might not be able to live without.

The word *cosmetic* covers a range of substances. A cosmetic can be anything that is applied to the human body for beautifying, cleaning, coloring, or preserving. It includes everything from lipstick and nail polish to bath oil and hair dye. Bath soap, antiperspirants, and dandruff shampoo are not considered cosmetics. These fall under the category of drugs. In 1938, the U.S. government enacted the Food, Drug, and Cosmetic Act. It states that drugs must be proven safe and effective before they can be sold. Cosmetics do not have to be proven effective, but many are tested for safety. As for the claims that a particular cream will make you look younger or a particular scent will attract a mate, that remains to be seen.

In the previous chapter, we discussed how detergents are used for cleaning many things, including dishes, clothing, floors, and cars. What most people don't realize is that detergents also are used when we brush our teeth. Most modern brands of toothpaste are nothing more than a detergent mixed with grit and flavor. In **Experiment 22:** *Testing Toothpaste*, you will examine these cosmetics and see which properties help to keep your pearly whites shining bright.

# EXPERIMENT 22 Testing Toothpaste

## Topic

What are some of the important properties of toothpaste?

## Introduction

Toothpaste is one of the cosmetics that people use every day. Even though its main function is to clean teeth, many brands also claim to strengthen teeth, freshen breath, control tartar, and whiten teeth. Toothpaste helps to remove plaque. Plaque is a sticky material that covers the teeth. It is made of bacteria and bits of food. The bacteria eat carbohydrates left in your mouth after you eat. They then give off acids that weaken the tooth enamel. If plaque isn't removed on a regular basis, it can form tartar. Tartar not only irritates the gums, but also could lead to tooth decay and gum disease. In order for a substance to be effective as toothpaste, it must remove plaque and clean stains from your teeth created by foods and beverages. In this activity, you will test several toothpaste formulas to determine their properties.

## Time Required

30 minutes preparation, 30 minutes for the experiment

## Materials

- hard-bristled toothbrush
- small, clear plastic disposable drinking cup
- baking soda
- gel-type toothpaste
- paste-type toothpaste
- piece of old, white cotton cloth from an old T-shirt or pillowcase
- grape juice or black coffee

- large bowl

- masking tape

- marking pen

- water

- watch or timer

- paper towels

> **Safety Note** When staining the white cotton fabric, make sure not to stain any clothing or furniture. Please review and follow the safety guidelines before proceeding.

## Procedure

1. Before conducting the experiment, stain a piece of white cotton fabric with either grape juice or black coffee. Use scissors to cut the fabric into a large square about 6 in. (15 cm) on a side. Place the fabric in the bottom of a bowl and allow it to soak in the liquid for at least 15 minutes. Periodically check on the fabric until it shows a distinct color change. Wring out the excess moisture and allow the fabric to dry for about 15 minutes. Dispose of the remaining liquid by dumping it down the sink drain.

2. Wrap a long piece of masking tape around the top of the plastic cup. Use the marker to label four places on the tape: "water," "baking soda," "gel," and "paste." The setup should look similar to Figure 1.

3. Wet the toothbrush with water and brush the outside of the cup directly under the place labeled "water." Brush up and down in the same location 25 times.

4. Rewet the toothbrush and dip the bristles in baking soda. Repeat the brushing procedure used in Step 3 under the label that says "baking soda." Clean the toothbrush thoroughly with water and then repeat the procedure two more times with the paste and gel. After you have finished, clean the toothbrush and then wipe any residue off the outside of the cup with a wet paper towel. Observe the outside of the cup and compare any marks left by the toothbrush under each label.

5. Use the marker to label four areas of the stained cloth with the same labels as you used in Step 2. Dip the toothbrush in plain water and, under the label for "water," brush the fabric in the same location 25 times.

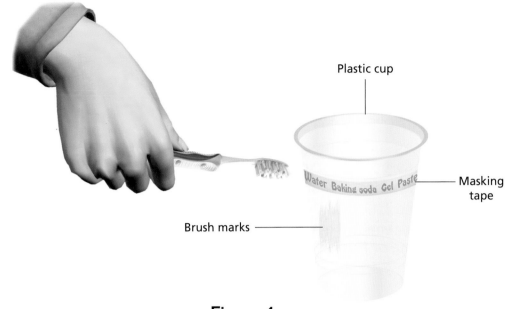

**Figure 1**

© Infobase Publishing

6. Rewet the toothbrush and dip it in the baking soda. Repeat the procedure in Step 5, this time under the label for "baking soda." Clean the tooth-brush thoroughly with water and then repeat the procedure two more times with the paste and gel. After you have finished, clean the toothbrush and then rinse the cloth under clean water. Allow the cloth to dry for about five minutes and then observe the areas under the labels. Compare any differences that you see.

## Analysis

1. What property of toothpaste were you testing in Steps 3 and 4?
2. What property of toothpaste were you testing in Steps 5 and 6?
3. Which substance scratched the cup the most?
4. Which substance removed the most stain from the fabric?
5. What was the reason for using plain water for each test?

## What's Going On?

To be effective, a good toothpaste has to be abrasive enough to remove plaque and have a strong enough cleaning agent to remove stains. The act of brushing by itself will clean teeth, but plain water is not great at removing stains. Baking soda, which has the chemical name sodium bicarbonate, has been used traditionally as a tooth cleaner over the years. It is mildly abrasive and does a better job than plain water but does not really have the stain-removing properties of a strong detergent. Most commercial toothpastes include harder abrasives, such as calcium carbonate or calcite and titanium dioxide. Of course it is important that toothpaste not be too abrasive because you don't want it to remove the enamel from your teeth.

In order to remove stains, most commercial toothpastes include both a detergent and some sort of bleaching agent. One of the most common is hydrogen peroxide. Simply having a paste made from detergent and grit would taste terrible in your mouth. That's why most commercial toothpastes also include flavorings and sweeteners in their recipes.

## Our Findings

1. The properties of abrasiveness and the ability to remove plaque.
2. The properties of the detergent or cleansing ability.
3. The answer will vary, but water and plain baking soda should show the fewest number of scratches.
4. The answer will vary, but water should be least effective at removing the stain.
5. Water acted as a control substance with which the other substances could be compared.

## PROTECTING SKIN BY KEEPING MOISTURE IN

Most people take their skin for granted. Yet, skin is incredibly important to our health and well-being. Skin serves several important functions. It acts as a waterproof covering for the body. It is the largest sensory organ, capable of detecting slight changes in temperature, pressure, and texture. Skin also provides the first line of defense against many of the germs that we encounter. Plus, it helps to regulate internal body temperature.

Most skin is made of two main layers. The outermost layer is called the epidermis. It has a layer of dead cells on top that are constantly being replaced by a thin layer of living cells underneath. Below the epidermis is the dermis, which is made of living skin cells. The dermis contains all of the nerves and blood vessels that keep the skin functioning. The dermis also contains special

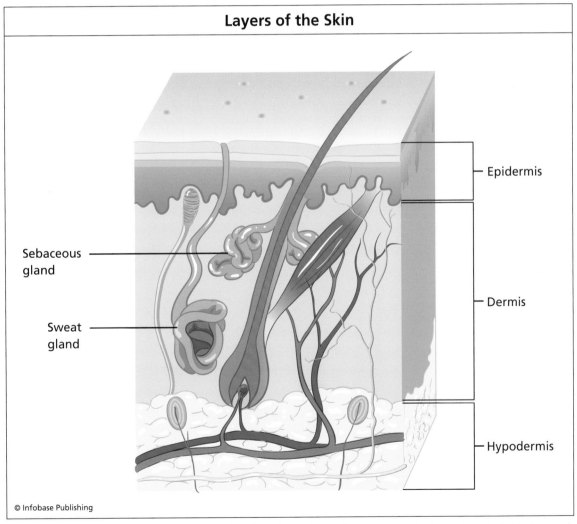

**Layers of the Skin**

Sebaceous gland

Sweat gland

Epidermis

Dermis

Hypodermis

© Infobase Publishing

A cross-sectional view of skin shows the dermis, epidermis, and sweat gland. The total thickness of the layers shown is approximately 0.08 inches (2 mm).

glands that secrete an oily substance called sebum. This keeps the skin moist and **elastic**. If the epidermis were to dry out, the living skin cells below would begin to die and the skin would become painful and start to crack. One way to help protect the skin from drying too much is to use moisturizing lotions and ointments. In **Experiment 23:** *Testing the Effects of Moisturizers*, you will see which type of skin treatment works best for holding moisture in the skin.

# EXPERIMENT 23

# Testing the Effects of Moisturizers

## Topic

How effective are different moisturizers at keeping skin from drying out?

## Introduction

The skin that covers your body is a complex sensory organ made up of several layers of cells, each providing a different function. The outermost layer of skin is called the epidermis. It is composed of a combination of dead cells (known as the *corneal layer*) and living cells. The dead cells are removed as you rub against clothing and other surfaces. The living cells replace the dead cells as they are lost. The corneal layer is made primarily from a material called keratin, which is a tough, fibrous protein. Keratin also is found in hair and fingernails, as well as feathers. In order for the skin to function properly, the keratin needs a moisture content of about 10%. Under normal circumstances, this ideal level of moisture is maintained by natural skin oils that are secreted by cells in the dermis, the layer of skin found below the epidermis. When skin is exposed to sun or wind, or when it is washed too often, these natural skin oils are removed and the corneal layer dries out. In these situations, people often use ointments and lotions on their skin to help keep the moisture in. In this activity, you are going to test three types of moisturizer to see which works best at minimizing moisture loss.

## Time Required

40 minutes

## Materials

- four fresh, whole baby spinach or basil leaves
- piece of aluminum foil about 12 in. (30 cm) long
- masking tape
- marker

- oven or toaster oven

- piece of white copier paper

- paper towels

- bottle of baby oil (mineral oil)

- bottle of moisturizing lotion (Vaseline Intensive Care, Jergens, or similar brand)

- jar of white petroleum jelly

- oven mitt

- timer or watch

- adult to assist you

**Safety Note**  Be careful not to get any of the lotions or oil on your clothes or furniture. If you do spill any of the products, use a damp paper towel and detergent to clean it up immediately. Use an oven mitt when removing the foil from the oven. It is recommended that you conduct this activity under the supervision of a responsible adult.

## Procedure

1. Roll up one sleeve to expose the skin on the back of one arm. Put a few drops of baby oil on one finger of the opposite hand and rub it into the skin of your arm. Observe how it behaves. Clean your finger with a paper towel. On another place on your arm, repeat the procedure with a drop of moisturizing lotion and then a dab of petroleum jelly. Compare the way each of the three substances feels and reacts with the skin. Record your results on the data table.

2. Turn a sheet of white copy paper on its side and write the words *baby oil, lotion,* and *petroleum jelly* across the top. Place a few drops of baby oil under the words *baby oil* and rub them into the paper with your finger. Clean your finger with a paper towel and repeat the procedure with the lotion and petroleum jelly under the proper labels. When you are finished, hold the paper up to the light and compare the three spots. Record your observations on the data table.

3. Set the oven or toaster oven to 200°F (93°C) and allow it to warm for a few minutes. Place four pieces of masking tape across the top of the foil. Give each one a label: "control," "baby oil," "lotion," and "petroleum jelly." Take one leaf and put a few drops of baby oil on the front and back surfaces.

Spinach leaves coated with moisturizers          Aluminum foil

**Figure 1**

© Infobase Publishing

Rub the oil in gently with your fingers and place the leaf on the foil under the proper label. Repeat the procedure with two additional leaves, coating one with lotion and the second with petroleum jelly. Place an untreated leaf under the label that says "control." Carefully place the sheet of foil in the oven and close the door. Allow the leaves to warm for 10 minutes and then use the oven mitt to remove the foil. After the leaves cool for a minute, pick up each one. Observe the texture and moisture content. Record your observations on the data table.

| Data Table 1 | | | | |
|---|---|---|---|---|
| | **Control** | **Baby Oil** | **Lotion** | **Petroleum Jelly** |
| Effect on skin | | | | |
| Effect on paper | | | | |
| Effect on fresh leaf | | | | |
| Effect on leaf after drying | | | | |

## Analysis

1. How did each of the moisturizers feel on your skin when you rubbed them in?
2. Which moisturizer was absorbed the fastest by your skin?
3. Which moisturizer was absorbed the fastest by the paper?
4. How did each leaf react to the moisturizers?
5. What was the purpose of having the untreated leaf as the control?
6. What was the effect of each moisturizer on the leaves after they were heated?

## What's Going On?

Dry, chapped skin can be a problem, especially in cold weather. When this happens, skin can develop painful cracks, feel sore to the touch, and look red, scaly, and unattractive. Repeated dryness can leave skin looking tough and leathery. In the United States alone, people spend billions of dollars each year on products designed to protect and moisturize the skin. If you take a careful look at the labels on most of these products, you'll find that they all tend to contain the same basic ingredients, including some type of mineral oil and petroleum jelly. Both of these products help to conserve and/or restore moisture, but they work in slightly different ways.

Both mineral oil and petroleum jelly are man-made materials derived from crude oil. They belong to a group of chemicals called alkanes. The main difference between the two is that at room temperature, petroleum jelly is a gooey, paste-like solid, while mineral oil is a thick, viscous liquid. Both compounds act as emollients: substances that help to soften the skin. Because they are oil-based, they seal in moisture to different degrees. Petroleum jelly is a semisolid paste, so it tends to lie on top of the skin, sealing pores and blocking the flow of moisture. You saw this with the both leaf and the paper. The petroleum jelly took a long time to soak into the paper, and it sealed the leaf so well that when the leaf was heated, it actually cooked in its own juices. The baby oil (which is simply mineral oil with added fragrances) soaked right into the paper and the leaf. While it did keep the leaf a little softer when it was exposed to the heat, the leaf still dried.

The substance that worked the best at keeping the leaf moist was the lotion. If you read the label closely, you'll probably find that it contains both mineral oil and petroleum jelly. It has the best properties of both substances.

## Our Findings

1. The oil soaked in right away. The lotion soaked in after rubbing. The jelly left a layer on top of the skin.

2. The oil was absorbed the fastest.

3. The oil was absorbed the fastest.

4. The oil soaked into the leaf and so did the lotion. The jelly coated the leaf, but didn't really soak into it.

5. The untreated leaf was a "control" to show what would happen with no moisturizer.

6. The leaf with the baby oil dried the most. The lotion-covered leaf kept many of the properties of the fresh leaf. The jelly-covered leaf appeared cooked and shriveled.

## ACIDS AND BASES IN THE MEDICINE CABINET

In the previous chapter, we introduced the pH scale and discussed how many of the substances that we use as cleaning agents around the house are chemically classified as bases. We also learned that common liquids, such as vinegar and lemon juice, are acids. As it turns out, acids and bases are not just found under kitchen cabinets and in the laundry room. They also appear in the medicine cabinet. Many of the common pills and preparations that people take to relieve pain, treat a cold, settle the stomach, or get rid of a headache belong in these two chemical groups. These include things such as milk of magnesia, a base; vitamin C, which is technically called ascorbic acid; and aspirin, which is acetylsalicylic acid. Occasionally, people take medicines known as antacids. In **Experiment 24:** *Testing the Effectiveness of Antacids*, you will discover what type of chemical these medications are and learn how they work.

# EXPERIMENT 24

# Testing the Effectiveness of Antacids

## Topic

What type of chemical is an antacid and how does it work?

## Introduction

Many of the substances that we encounter in our daily lives can be classified as either acids or bases. These compounds are chemical opposites. When they are mixed, each neutralizes the other. One place that you can find a powerful acid is inside your own body. To help break down food during digestion, your stomach produces a substance called hydrochloric acid. When you consume too many acidic foods (such as soda, tomato sauce, or lemonade) or are under stress, the level of acid in your stomach becomes too great. This makes you develop hyperacidity, also called acid indigestion or heartburn. To help reduce the level of acid in the stomach, people take a variety of antacids. They are sold under many brand names, and come in liquids or tablets. In this activity, you are going to test three brands of antacids and discover why they help to put out the fire of heartburn.

## Time Required

60 minutes

## Materials

- small head of red cabbage (fresh, not preserved)
- electric blender
- metal strainer
- large measuring cup
- 3 brands of antacid tablets (Rolaids, Tums, Maalox, etc.), each containing 1,000 mg calcium carbonate
- 7 large (16 oz, or 500 mL) clear plastic disposable cups

- ¼ cup (60 mL) measuring cup
- water
- paper towels
- 4 plastic teaspoons
- bottle of white vinegar
- box of baking soda
- masking tape
- marker
- adult to assist you

**Safety Note** If you spill any of the cabbage juice, you should use a damp paper towel to clean it up immediately. It is recommended that you conduct this activity under the supervision of a responsible adult.

## Procedure

1. Fill the blender ¾ full of cold, fresh water. Tear off four or five leaves from the cabbage and place them in the blender. Put the top on the blender and turn it on the highest speed for about 30 seconds or until all of the cabbage leaves are chopped into a fine pulp. The water should be a dark purple color.

2. Use the tape and marker to label four plastic cups: "vinegar," "baking soda," "mixture," and "plain cabbage juice." Label the other three cups with the names of the three antacids that you are using.

3. Carefully remove the top section of the blender and pour the cabbage juice through the strainer into the large measuring cup. Fill each cup *except* the cup that is labeled "mixture" with ¼ cup (60 mL) of cabbage juice. Next, add ¼ cup (60 mL) of plain water to each of the cups with cabbage juice. This will dilute the cabbage juice; it should look light purple in color.

4. Add ¼ cup (60 mL) white vinegar to the proper cup. Vinegar is an acid. Observe the color that the cabbage juice turns. Next, add 1 teaspoon (5 mL) of baking soda to the proper cup. Baking soda is a base. Stir the baking soda until it dissolves, and observe the color of the cabbage juice. Pour ½ of the cup labeled "vinegar" into the cup labeled "mixture." Add ½ of the cup labeled "baking soda" to the cup labeled "mixture," and observe what happens when the acid and base mix.

**Figure 1**

© Infobase Publishing

5. Add ¼ cup (60 mL) vinegar to each of the cups labeled with the names of the antacids. The liquid should look like the liquid in the cup labeled "vinegar." Add one antacid tablet to each cup, matching the brands to the cups. Allow the tablets to dissolve for 15 to 20 minutes. Then gently stir each cup with a teaspoon to help the tablet dissolve. Compare the color of the solutions in the cups to the cups labeled "vinegar" and "plain cabbage juice."

## Analysis

1. What color did the vinegar (acid) turn the cabbage juice?
2. What color did the baking soda (base) turn the cabbage juice?
3. What happened when you mixed the cabbage juice solutions with vinegar and baking soda together?  What does this mean?
4. What happened to the color of the vinegar/cabbage juice solutions when you added the antacids and they finally dissolved?
5. Based on your observations, which brand of antacid worked best to neutralize the acid found in the vinegar?

## What's Going On?

People have been trying to come up with treatments for hyper-acidity for thousands of years. Once chemists began understanding how acid/base reactions worked, they were able to get a handle on the problem and come up with more effective treatments. The best way to treat the symptoms of hyperacidity is to neutralize the extra stomach acid with some type of base. Almost any type of base will do. Early on, the treatment that was most often used to relieve heartburn was to drink a mixture of baking soda and water. As you discovered in your experiment, when the cup with the baking soda was mixed with the cup with the vinegar, the cabbage juice returned to its original purple color. This meant that the baking soda had neutralized the acid. You should have also noticed that when the two solutions mixed, they produced foam. One of the major disadvantages of using baking soda to cure hyperacidity is that it releases a great deal of carbon dioxide gas, which tends to make a person burp.

Many commercial antacid tablets use calcium carbonate to neutralize stomach acid. The three antacids that you used all had the same amount of calcium carbonate (1,000 mg), so they all wound up working about the same. Calcium carbonate is a variety of chalk. Ingesting too much may lead to constipation. That's why some manufacturers also include magnesium compounds in their formulas. Magnesium is a laxative; in large dosages, it can lead to diarrhea. So the antacid chalk and the magnesium cancel each other out, leading to a reduction in acid with no extra stomach distress!

## Our Findings

1. The vinegar turned the cabbage juice reddish pink.
2. The baking soda turned it blue-green.
3. The color changed back to the purple color of the plain cabbage juice. This meant that the vinegar and baking soda canceled each other or neutralized each other.
4. As they dissolved, the tablets began to change the color of the solutions from pink to purple.
5. Answers will vary, but in the end, all of the mixtures should have looked about the same, meaning that they all worked about equally well. The only major difference should have been how quickly they changed color.

## FUNGUS AMONG US

It can happen without warning. You're on a basketball court about to take a free throw, or at a bowling alley lining up a spare. As you try to concentrate on the game, your mind is suddenly taken over by an itching, burning sensation in your feet. No matter how hard you try to ignore it, the pain gets worse until you just want to rip off your sneakers and scratch. You have become another unsuspecting victim of athlete's foot!

If you've ever suffered from athlete's foot, you know that it can be one of the most irritating types of medical conditions. Athlete's foot is caused by a fungus that rapidly grows in warm, moist places, such as between your toes or on the soles of your feet. It is a problem especially in warm weather, when people spend lots of time wearing sweaty running shoes, soccer cleats, or basketball sneakers. Left untreated, feet can itch and burn, and the skin between the toes and on the bottom of the feet can peel. While athlete's foot is not a life-threatening condition, it can be annoying. It also can lead to complications if not treated. In **Experiment 25:** *Stopping Fungal Growth,* you will test several common remedies for athlete's foot to see which is best at stopping the dreaded fungus among us.

# Stopping Fungal Growth

## Topic

What's the most effective way to stop the growth of fungus?

## Introduction

Fungi are simple organisms that unlike green plants, cannot make their own food. Many types of fungus are saprophytes. They live off dead organisms, such as leaves, rotting wood, or—in the case of the athlete's foot fungus— dead skin cells on the bottom of a person's foot. Most fungi thrive in warm, dark, damp areas, such as the inside of a sweaty tennis sneaker. Not all

**Figure 1**

fungi are bad. Some helpful fungi include yeast, mushrooms, and the mold from which penicillin is made. For humans, fungal infections are common and painful. They can cause rashes, peeling skin, and severe itching. It can take several weeks to get an infection under control. Over the years, many methods have been used to stop fungal growth. In this activity, you will compare three methods to see which works best. Instead of trying them out on a human subject, you will run your tests on a slice of bread. The fungus you will try to stop is common bread mold.

## Time Required

30 minutes for preparation, 2 weeks for observation

## Materials

- 4 slices of bread without preservatives, all from the same loaf

- 4 zip-top sandwich bags

- baby powder made from 100% cornstarch

- spray bottle of soapy water

- can of Tinactin or similar brand athlete's foot treatment. It must say "antifungal" on the label.

- spray bottle of plain water

- masking tape

- paper towels

- marker

- warm, dark area (closet or out-of-the-way shelf)

**Safety Note** When doing this activity at home, make certain that other family members are aware that the bread in the bags has been treated with chemicals and should not be eaten. It is recommended that you conduct this activity under the supervision of a responsible adult.

## Procedure

1.  Lay the four slices of bread on a paper towel. Use the spray bottle filled with water to gently mist each slice of bread. Do *not* soak the bread. Allow the slices of bread to stand in the open for about 15 minutes.

2.  Put a large piece of masking tape on the outside of each sandwich bag. Across the top of each piece of tape write: "Science Experiment in Progress: Do not disturb!" Then on one piece of tape, write "control: water only." (*Control* means "unchanged" in the language of scientific testing.) Put a piece of bread in this bag and zip the bag closed.

3.  Write "baby powder" on another bag. Sprinkle a light dusting of baby powder over the top of a piece of bread. Place it in this bag and seal the bag. Wash and dry your hands.

4.  Write "soap solution" on a bag. Spray a piece of bread lightly with the detergent solution. Place it in the bag and seal it. Wash and dry your hands.

5.  Write "antifungal spray" on the last bag. Spray the last piece of bread with a light covering of the athlete's foot spray. Place it in the bag and seal it. Wash and dry your hands and dispose of the paper towel.

6.  Place the bags with the bread slices together in a warm, dark location where they will not be disturbed. Allow them to sit for five days. On day six, observe the bread for any sign of discoloration or mold growth. Record any changes to the bread that you see. Repeat this step every day until two weeks have passed.

## Analysis

1.  What was the purpose of the "control" in this experiment?
2.  Why did the bread all have to be from the same loaf?
3.  Why did all the bread have to be stored together?
4.  Which piece of bread developed the mold the fastest?
5.  Which piece of bread developed the least mold?

### What's Going On?

Fungi come in many forms and are found in almost every part of the environment. Most fungi reproduce by means of microscopic spores that freely float in the air. Once they settle on a surface with the right conditions, they begin to grow and reproduce. Athlete's foot is caused by a fungus named *Trichophyton mentagrophytes.* Even though this is not the same type of fungus as bread mold, both thrive in warm, dark, damp conditions. In order to get rid of athlete's foot fungus, a person needs to wash the infected area regularly with soap and water. This removes the dead skin and surface fungus, but detergents alone usually do not kill fungus. Keeping the affected area dry also is a good idea, which is why many people use baby powder. The problem is that baby powder made from cornstarch might have fungal spores in it, and the fungus can use the cornstarch as a source of food. If powders are used, they should be made from 100% talcum, not cornstarch. The most effective way of killing a fungus is to use an antifungal cream or spray. These substances contain a fungicide, which is a specific man-made chemical designed to disrupt the life cycle of the fungus and keep it from coming back.

## Our Findings

1. The control is there to allow you to compare the mold growth on a piece of bread that had no treatment at all.
2. The bread should all come from the same loaf in order to ensure that each slice has the same composition.
3. All of the bread slices had to be stored together so that they were exposed to the same environmental conditions.
4. Either the control or the slice of bread treated with the baby powder should have grown the most mold.
5. The bread treated with the antifungal spray should have had almost no mold on it.

## A FINAL WORD OF WARNING

We've only begun to scratch the surface when it comes to identifying man-made products used on or in the human body. It is important to remember that apart from food and drugs, many of the products that we use on our bodies are not regulated and do not have to undergo regular testing. In many cases, manufacturers can make claims about the benefit of a product, and you have no way of knowing if they are true. Even some of the products that have been tested and deemed safe can cause physical problems if they are used too frequently or improperly. Before using any products on or in your body, read the labels to see what they contain. Follow directions closely. After all, you only have one body, and while beauty may only be skin deep, you want to keep that skin intact!

# 6

# What the Future Holds

Throughout the first five chapters, we've taken a look at some of the major groups of man-made materials and the ways they are used. We haven't touched on other categories, such as ceramics, fuels, and food. Because the science of chemistry is evolving so quickly, it's hard to know what materials will be available for us to use next year, let alone in the next decade or the next century. There have been a number of recent developments in materials science that give a glimpse at what the future holds. Some developments may promise a better world, while others serve as warnings for problems that we are going to have to face. Here are a few issues and ideas that you might want to keep track of. First, some bad news…

## THE GROWTH OF SUPER GERMS

These days, you might hear stories on the news about flesh-eating bacteria, the return of tuberculosis, and the growth of "super germs" that infect people and cannot be killed by even the most powerful drugs. Even though these stories may sound like science fiction, the problems are real. We are having these problems now due to our misuse of some man-made substances that we have depended on for the last century.

The whole story begins about 150 years ago in the United Kingdom. If you were a patient about to check into a hospital for surgery back then, your chances of coming out alive were probably worse than if you never went into the hospital at all. That's because the concept of a germ didn't exist. When surgeons operated, not only didn't they wear masks and gloves, but they also didn't even wash their hands. Even worse, they often used the same surgical instruments on a few patients in a row without cleaning or sterilizing them. This all began to change in the 1860s when a doctor named Joseph Lister began trying a new approach.

Lister was put in charge of the surgical wing of Scotland's Glasgow Royal Infirmary in 1861. He was stunned by the number of patients who died after surgery. What was even stranger was the fact that the patients weren't dying from their wounds. What was killing them more often than not was a condition called sepsis, or hospital fever. No one could come up with a cause for this strange disease, although there were many wild theories. Trained as a scientist, Lister began reading the literature and came across the work of Louis Pasteur. In 1856, Pasteur had discovered that food and wine could spoil because of tiny organisms that were too small to see without a microscope. Lister wondered if these so-called "microbes" could be making people sick.

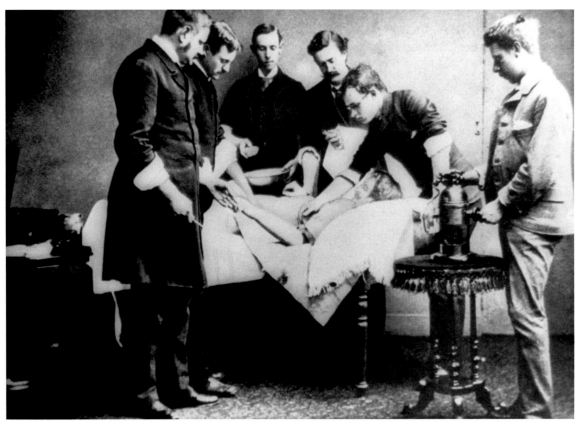

An 1883 surgery utilizes antiseptic methods thanks to work done by Dr. Joseph Lister. Lister found that crude phenol solution (carbolic acid) could be used as an antiseptic for dressings or instruments and as a spray in the operating room. The instrument on the right sprays the antiseptic into the air.

Lister started ordering doctors to wash their hands before surgery, and began spraying the operating rooms with carbolic acid to kill the potential germs. He called his technique antisepsis, and within a few months, the death rate after surgery dropped from more than 50% to less than 15%. Later, different solutions using alcohol and similar chemicals were developed for killing germs on wounds. This led to the development of products that we use today called antiseptics and antibacterial agents.

If you look at most detergents, cleaners, and sanitary wipes sold today, they generally say "antibacterial" on them. We use these products everywhere—hand sanitizers can even be found available for free in supermarkets and libraries. You would think that with all the antiseptics being used today, there would be no germs left on the planet, but you would be wrong! Now back to our story.

Fast-forward to the year 1928. Scientists and doctors are now very familiar with germs, microbes, and bacteria. They use antiseptics to clean wounds and surfaces, and surgeons wash their hands and sterilize their instruments. However, people are still getting sick from mysterious infections. British microbiologist Alexander Fleming was growing a type of bacteria called staphylococci on a glass dish when he noticed that some mold had also begun to grow on the dish. When he looked closely, he saw that the bacteria were not growing near the mold. In fact, the mold seemed to be killing the bacteria. The type of mold was a common bread mold called *Penicillium chrysogenun.* Fleming wrote down his discovery but never really followed up with it. Ten years later, two other scientists found Fleming's work and used his discovery to create penicillin, the world's first antibiotic.

When penicillin was first introduced, doctors finally had a substance that could cure bacterial infections. They even referred to it as a "magic bullet." Over the last 60 years, penicillin and other antibiotics have saved millions of lives. Early on, there were only a few antibiotics available, and they were very expensive to make. As a result, they were usually reserved for those people who were critically ill. As chemists unlocked the structure of antibiotic compounds, however, they became easier and cheaper to produce. Use skyrocketed. Not only were doctors prescribing them to patients who were extremely ill, but they began using them prophylactically, which meant that they would be given out to patients to prevent infection even before they got sick. The problem was compounded further by the fact that farmers and ranchers began giving the same antibiotics to their farm animals to keep them from getting sick. Soon, people started noticing that the antibiotics weren't working as well as they once did. People who had bacterial infections needed bigger doses and stronger antibiotics to knock out the germs. The scientists and doctors hadn't counted on something: evolution.

Although antiseptics and antibiotics kill bacteria and other germs, they don't kill them all. If you've ever read the label on one of those hand sanitizers, it says that the sanitizer kills 99% of germs on contact. Have you ever wondered what happens to the other 1%? They live and multiply. They live because they have a natural resistance to the chemicals in the sanitizer. They pass on this resistance to their descendants, creating more resistant bacteria.

If an organism survives long enough to reproduce, it will pass on its traits, or characteristics. If bacteria can survive a bout with an antibiotic, they will pass on this resistance when they reproduce. Gradually, the number of drug-resistant bacteria in the environment increases.

When scientists first became aware of the problem of antibiotic resistance, they began creating more powerful antibiotics. At first, they kept ahead of the bacteria, killing off all but the most resistant germs. But once again, they didn't get them all. The germs kept evolving, and the scientists kept creating stronger antibiotics and antiseptics. Bacteria appear to have a great ability to adapt to new drugs. It's beginning to look like we're starting to lose the race. So what do we do?

The answer is not a simple one, but it does involve some common sense. Scientists already have come up with some superantibiotics that seem to work on even the most resistant forms of bacteria. As with the very first antibiotics, they are very expensive and difficult to produce. In order to break the cycle of antibiotic-resistant bacteria, however, these new antibiotics cannot be used haphazardly. In fact, many scientists and doctors have said that antibiotics should be reserved for only severe infections. Furthermore, there is a movement to phase out the activity of giving antibiotics to farm animals to prevent infections. By working to reverse the trend of resistant bacteria, doctors may be able to keep a magic bullet in reserve to fight off super germs well into the future.

## CERAMIC HIPS

The news concerning man-made materials and the medical profession isn't all bad. Over the last few decades, materials scientists have teamed up with doctors to create some amazing replacement parts. One of the most common is an artificial hip, which is designed to replace a natural joint that has worn out due to the effects of arthritis.

Arthritis affects millions of people. It starts as an inflammation of a joint. Over time, it can cause cartilage to wear away. Cartilage covers the ends of bones at joints. It allows them to move past each other smoothly. Once the cartilage has been destroyed, the bones begin to rub against one another. This reduces the range of motion in the joint and causes pain.

For many people, arthritis of the hip is so severe that they choose to have the natural hip joint replaced with an artificial one. In a traditional hip replacement surgery, a metal rod is inserted into the patient's femur, or thighbone. At the top of the rod is a metal ball, which is usually made from a superstrong cobalt chrome molybdenum alloy. The combination of metals used in this is alloy is designed to be long lasting and "inert" so it won't be rejected by a person's immune system. The ball makes up one side of the joint. On the other side of the joint is a plastic liner (usually made from polyethylene) shaped like a socket. The ball fits into this socket. The plastic liner is attached to a metal shell, which is in turn cemented to the patient's pelvis.

Surgeons have been replacing hip joints for more than 40 years. One problem is that the replacement parts wear out, especially in younger patients who are very active. In some cases, small pieces of polyethylene from the liner are attacked by the body's own immune system, leading to a condition called osteolysis. In this condition, the bone around the implant dissolves. Then the entire artificial joint must be replaced. Because of advances in the production of new superceramics,

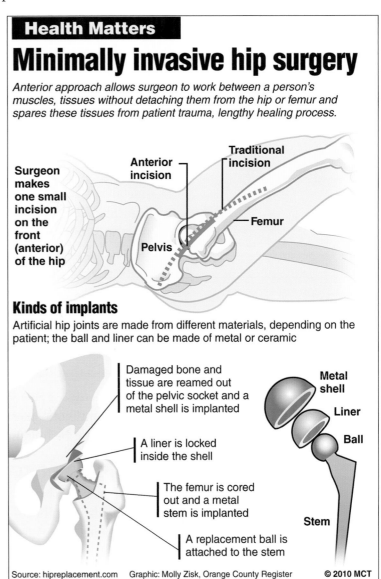

### Health Matters
# Minimally invasive hip surgery

*Anterior approach allows surgeon to work between a person's muscles, tissues without detaching them from the hip or femur and spares these tissues from patient trauma, lengthy healing process.*

Traditional incision

Anterior incision

Surgeon makes one small incision on the front (anterior) of the hip

Pelvis

Femur

### Kinds of implants

Artificial hip joints are made from different materials, depending on the patient; the ball and liner can be made of metal or ceramic

Damaged bone and tissue are reamed out of the pelvic socket and a metal shell is implanted

A liner is locked inside the shell

The femur is cored out and a metal stem is implanted

A replacement ball is attached to the stem

Metal shell

Liner

Ball

Stem

Source: hipreplacement.com    Graphic: Molly Zisk, Orange County Register    © 2010 MCT

New materials and techniques help make hip surgery less invasive so patients can regain use of their hips in less time and with fewer side effects.

doctors now have a new choice of materials when it comes to hip replacement parts.

People tend to associate ceramics with pottery, glassware, and floor tiles. Ceramics are materials that are made from clay and other earth materials that have been fired at a high temperature. During the firing process, the individual particles fuse to various degrees, resulting in a product with a unique set of properties. In the case of glass, silica (sand) is used as a starting material. When glass is made, the silica melts and forms a liquid, which then cools into a solid. One of the drawbacks of traditional ceramics is that they tend to be brittle and fragile. When you drop a wine glass or a piece of pottery on a hard surface, it will shatter. Over the past few decades, however, materials scientists have been creating a new breed of ceramics that are stronger than steel! One of these products is a special type of oxide called zirconia, which is being used in place of steel and plastic in artificial hip joints.

All artificial joints will wear over time. A traditional implant—made from a metal ball and polyethylene liner—wears down about 0.1 mm each year. This means that the replacement joint could last an average of 10 to 15 years. Instead of having a metal ball, the new implants have a ceramic ball in a polyethylene liner. The ceramic material is much harder than metal and is scratch resistant. Because the ceramics have an ultrasmooth surface, the wear rates on the polyethylene liners are estimated to be about 0.05 mm each year, about half as much as with the metal balls. Lower rates of wear mean that the implant will last longer and produce less debris in the joint. This means that there will be less of a chance of a patient developing osteolysis.

Over the past two decades, surgeons in Europe have been experimenting with a hip joint that has a ceramic ball and a ceramic liner. In this new system, the wear rates are estimated to be as low as 0.0001 mm a year. With rates this low, the joint will outlast the patient!

## PLASTICS FROM CORN

As we saw in Chapter 4, plastics are an important part of our world. They can be found in everything from packaging to hip replacements, and it would be difficult to live without them. Plastics do have two major problems that have had scientists scrambling for solutions. Most modern plastics are made from polymers that are derived from petroleum, or oil. Crude oil is a thick, gooey liquid found under the ground. It forms from the slow decomposition of organisms that were buried and trapped in layers of sediment millions of years ago. Over the years, the heat and pressure under the ground slowly "cooked" the organisms, turning them into oil. Because oil takes so long to form naturally, it is considered to be a nonrenewable resource. In other words, once it is used up, it's gone and can't be replaced.

Petroleum is used for more than plastics. It is also the top source of transportation fuel. It is used to make gasoline for cars, diesel fuel for trucks and trains, and jet fuel for planes. Oil also is used to heat homes, run factories, and make electricity in power plants. With so many demands for petroleum, the big question is, can we continue to use it to make plastics? It is estimated that in the United States alone, almost 200,000 barrels of oil a day are used just to make conventional plastic packaging material. This seems to be a big waste of a resource on something that gets immediately thrown out.

NatureWorks makes plastic and fibers from plants. Their factories run plant sugars through a fermentation process to make lactic acid. Then they polymerize the lactic acid and create a biopolymer resin pellet called Ingeo, which is sold to converters around the world that melt the resin to produce a film or thin sheet or fiber.

The second major problem with plastics is the fact that most are not biodegradable. Unlike products made from paper or wood, plastics take a very long time to disintegrate. Because of this, the amount of plastic waste in the world will continue to grow. It is estimated that plastics take up almost 25% of the space in landfills right now. At the rate that new plastic products are being developed, that percentage is sure to increase. As we discovered earlier, one possible solution to this problem is the recycling of plastics, but in reality, even the best plastic recycling programs wouldn't come close to recovering all of the plastic waste. Much of it would still wind up in landfills or as litter.

In an effort to solve both of these problems, materials scientists working in the plastics industries have come up with a novel solution that seems to be catching on. Instead of making plastic from a nonrenewable source, such as petroleum, why not make it from a renewable source, such as corn? Before you start choking on your taco chips, the idea is not as far-fetched as you might think. In fact, corn plastic has been around in labs for about 25 years. Its development has had to surpass several scientific hurdles, but it appears to be ready to roll. In fact, a

Nebraska company called NatureWorks LLC has been cranking out tons of corn-based plastic since 2003.

The product that NatureWorks makes is called Ingeo, and it's based on a type of plastic resin known as polylactic acid, or PLA. Instead of using the hydrocarbons in oil as a source material, PLA uses dextrose, a sugar extracted from starch. In theory, dextrose could be derived from many sources—including wheat, sugar beets, and sugarcane—but Nebraska is in the middle of corn country, so NatureWorks uses corn. The dextrose is fermented to make lactic acid, which is converted into a substance called lactide. The lactide molecules are linked into long polymer chains to make PLA. When it comes from the NatureWorks factory, PLA resin looks like little white plastic beads. From here, it is shipped to fabricators who turn it into films, wraps, fibers, and containers.

Because PLA uses corn as a source material, it reduces the demand for oil, but it does not eliminate it. Corn has to be grown, shipped, and processed. That takes tractors and trucks and machinery, all of which run on petroleum products. In addition, growing corn requires fertilizers, and fertilizers also are made primarily from—you guessed it—oil. But even when all of this oil use is taken into account, the amount needed to make PLA is far less than using oil to make plastic directly.

The other major advantage of PLA, at least in theory, is that it is biodegradable. Many containers made from PLA are stamped with the word *compostable*, suggesting that if they are placed in a backyard compost pile or bin, they will break down and turn into mulch. It turns out that this is not quite the case. Composting PLA must be done in a "controlled composting environment," usually found only in a large-scale industrial composting facility. If a container made from PLA is thrown into a landfill, it probably will last just as long as a PET soda bottle.

One other drawback with corn-based plastics is that they are very unstable at moderately high temperatures. Once the temperature gets over 114°F (46°C), they start to melt. This could be a real problem if you plan on spending a day at the beach, or if you leave your lunch sitting in a PLA container in a car on a hot summer day. Even with these problems, the use of bioplastics is on the rise, and most scientists feel that it's only a matter of time before they work out the problems of disposal and melting. Who knows, it may only be a matter of time before both your favorite brand of taco chips and the bag they come in are made from corn!

## FUELS FOR THE FUTURE

As we just discussed, one of the biggest problems that the world is facing is the long-term shortage of oil. By far, the biggest use of petroleum products is as fuel for cars, trucks, trains, and planes. For about 100 years, petroleum has been the main source of transportation fuels. Recent studies have shown that one serious side effect of burning petroleum-based fuels has been a steady increase in carbon dioxide in the air. Carbon dioxide, along with methane and a few other pollutants, are known as greenhouse gases. When they build up in the atmosphere, many scientists believe that it leads to global warming.

As the number of cars and trucks on the road continues to grow, the pressure to find an alternative source of transportation fuel has been mounting. In an attempt to stretch the remaining petroleum reserves and cut greenhouse gas emissions, many governments have required automakers to increase the fuel efficiency of their vehicles. The biggest boost in this area has come from the introduction of hybrid vehicles, which run on both gasoline and electricity. In some cases, these vehicles can go more than 50 miles (80 kilometers) on a single gallon of gas. Another area of hope is in the introduction of all-electric vehicles made possible by bigger and better batteries. Another area of research is revisiting an old concept known as **biofuels**.

Biofuels are not made from crude oil. They are made from plants, which use the process of photosynthesis to store solar energy as sugars in their cells. People have been making fuels from plants for thousands of years. In ancient times, people burned olive oil in their lamps and used peanut oil to run machinery. In fact, when Henry Ford first introduced his Model-T in the early 1900s, the plan was to use **ethanol** (a type of alcohol) as the fuel. This changed when large reservoirs of crude oil were found. Oil was cheap and plentiful, so the idea of using biofuels went back on the shelf. Today, scientists are dusting off the idea, and it's making a big comeback.

The truth is that all fuels, including gasoline and diesel, are biofuels. As we discussed earlier, crude oil is the end result of plants and animals that have been "processed" over millions of years by heat and pressure underneath the surface of the earth. When scientists make biofuels today, they are simply doing it a lot quicker.

Right now, the most common biofuel is ethanol, which is made mostly from corn and sugarcane. In the United States, almost all the gasoline we buy at the pump is actually a blend of gasoline and ethanol. This fuel goes by the name E10 because it is a mix of 10% ethanol and 90% gasoline. Using ethanol mixed with (or instead of) gasoline has several advantages. Because it comes from plants that are growing today, it is a renewable resource, rather than a fossil fuel. When mixed with gasoline, ethanol not only extends the amount of fuel available, but also burns cleaner, releasing far fewer greenhouse gases and other pollutants.

Ethanol is made by using yeast to convert sugars into alcohol by a process called fermentation. Fermentation is the same process used to make wine and beer. Within the next few years, ethanol production in the United States alone will exceed 12 billion gallons (45 billion liters) a year. The problem is that almost all (95%) of this ethanol comes from corn, which also is a source of food for people and animals. This has many world leaders concerned, especially because many countries of the world are already experiencing food shortages. In addition, it takes energy and resources to grow corn. Some scientists calculate that the energy needed to produce ethanol from corn exceeds the energy of the ethanol itself. If this is the case, then making ethanol would be worse, from an energy standpoint, than turning oil into gasoline.

Ethanol does not have to be made from corn. Almost any source of sugar or starch will do. In Brazil, for example, almost all ethanol comes from sugarcane. In Europe, it is made from sugar beets. Scientists would like to make ethanol from a non-food source, such as grass or sawdust. This is where cellulosic ethanol comes into play.

Cellulosic ethanol is alcohol produced from the structural parts of plant cells, rather than sugars or starches. Cellulose is a tough, fibrous material that makes up the cell walls of plants. It contains the same basic chemicals as sugar, but they are locked up tighter. Scientists believe that if they can break down cellulose into its component molecules, we will then have a virtually unlimited source of cheap material from which to make fuel. The problem is that cellulose is tough stuff. In recent years, there have been a number of breakthroughs using acids and enzymes to break it down. One process mimics what happens inside termites when they digest wood. It seems like it's only a matter of time before we are all driving around in biofuel-powered vehicles. On paper, at least, it seems like a perfect solution. When fuels burn, they release carbon dioxide into the air, but plants take carbon dioxide out of the air and use it to grow. It sounds like a win-win situation, brought to us by modern chemistry with a little help from photosynthesis and the sun!

# Glossary

**Adhesive**   A sticky material that can be used to bond objects together

**Alloy**   A metal made by mixing two or more metals together

**Biofuel**   A fuel made from plants

**Caulk**   Material used to fill gaps between wooden boards and to seal spaces around windows and doorways

**Cement**   Product made from limestone and clay that when mixed with water and allowed to dry turns into a solid, rocklike mass

**Corrosion**   The chemical process that occurs when a metal rusts (oxidizes)

**Cosmetic**   (noun) A substance used for beautifying the body

**Drywall**   A building material made from plaster and formed into sheets; also called sheetrock

**Ductile**   A property of a solid object; a ductile object can be hammered thin or bent into a variety of shapes without breaking.

**Elastic**   A property of a solid object; an elastic object changes shape due to a force but returns to its original shape when the force is released. A spring is elastic.

**Ethanol**   An alcohol used as a fuel made from plants

**Kiln**   A special high-temperature oven used for baking clay to make pottery

**Lath**   Closely spaced wooden boards onto which plaster is spread to make a wall

**Malleable**   A property of a solid object; a malleable object can be shaped by hammering or rolling.

**Monomer**   A small molecule that can be chemically linked to other molecules to form a polymer

**Mortar**   The type of cement used between bricks and stones

**Ore**   A rock or mineral that contains metal

**Oxidation**   A chemical reaction involving oxygen, including combustion and corrosion

**Particleboard**   Man-made wood product made from sawdust, wood flakes, and resins

**Plaster**    Substance made from the mineral gypsum that when mixed with water dries into a hard compound used for making casts and walls

**Plastic**    (adj.) A property of a solid object; a plastic object can be molded; (noun) a class of synthetic polymers used for a variety of products

**Plywood**    Wood product made from thin layers or "plies" of wood glued together

**Polymer**    A giant molecule composed of smaller chemical elements called monomers; most plastics and synthetic adhesives are polymers.

**Rust**    Corrosion of iron or steel

**Sheetrock**    See *Drywall*.

**sythetic fibers**    Fibers not taken from a natural source, such as cotton or wool

# Bibliography

Berkow, Robert, M.D., editor-in-chief. *The Merck Manual of Medical Information.* Whitehouse Station, N.J., Merck Research Laboratories, 1997.

Dittman, Richard and Glenn Schmeig. *Physics in Everyday Life.* New York: McGraw Hill, 1979.

Editors of Consumers Guide. *How Things Work.* Lincolnwood, Ill.: Publications International Ltd., 1994.

Hewitt, Paul. *Conceptual Physics, 8th Ed.* New York: Addison Wesley, 1998.

Hill, John. *Chemistry for Changing Times, 4th Ed.* Minneapolis: Burgess Publishing Co., 1984.

Hodges, Henry. *Technology in the Ancient World.* New York: Barnes & Noble Books, 1992.

Macaulay, David. *The Way Things Work.* Boston: Houghton Mifflin, 1988.

Mandell, Muriel. *Simple Kitchen Experiments.* New York: Sterling Publishing Co., 1993.

Suchocki, John. *Conceptual Chemistry.* New York: Addison Wesley, 2001.

Tomecek, Stephen M. *What a Great Idea! Inventions that Changed the World.* New York: Scholastic, 2002.

# Further Resources

Bardhan-Quallen, Sudipta. *Championship Science Fair Projects.* New York: Sterling Publishing Co., 2004.

Connolly, Sean. *The Book of Totally Irresponsible Science.* New York: Workman Publishing, 2008.

Oxlade, Chris. *How We Use Plastic.* Chicago: Raintree, 2004.

Slavin, Bill. *Transformed: How Everyday Things Are Made.* Tonawanda, N.Y.: Kids Can Press, 2005.

Tocci, Salvatore. *Experiments with Soap.* New York: Children's Press, 2003.

Tomecek, Stephen. *Electromagnetism, and How It Works.* New York: Chelsea House, 2007.

———. *What a Great Idea! Inventions that Changed the World.* New York: Scholastic, 2002.

VanCleave, Janice. *A+ Projects in Chemistry.* New York: John Wiley & Sons, 1993.

## Web Sites

**The American Ceramics Society Knowledge Center**
http://ceramics.org/knowledge-center/learn-about-ceramics/
*Ceramics is not just pottery and glassware. Ceramics are used in a range of industries, including aerospace, electronics, transportation, and even sports. If you want to learn more about the modern uses of ceramics, then this Web site is a great place to start.*

**American Chemistry Council Plastics Division**
http://www.americanchemistry.com/plastics/
*Maintained by the American Chemistry Council, this site provides a wealth of information about the many places where plastics are used in our world today. It includes links to many educational resources.*

**Materials Science & Engineering Laboratory**

http://www.nist.gov/msel/

*This Web site is maintained by the National Institute of Standards and Technology. It provides background information and links to the latest news stories about a range of man-made materials, including ceramics, polymers, and metallurgy.*

**Oak Ridge National Laboratory**

http://www.ornl.gov/

*The Oak Ridge National Laboratory is a government research center devoted to the exploration of new technologies in materials science and energy. Here you can learn about the latest developments in building efficiency, insulation standards, biofuels, advanced materials, and nanotechnology.*

**Toothpaste World**

http://www.toothpasteworld.com

*This Web site tells the story behind toothpaste, including its history and some interesting formulas that have been used over the years. It also provides many fun facts about toothpaste and gives helpful hints on selecting toothpastes for different situations.*

# Picture Credits

# Index

# About the Author

STEPHEN M. TOMECEK is a scientist who has written more than 30 nonfiction books for both children and teachers, including *Bouncing & Bending Light,* the 1996 winner of the American Institute of Physics Science Writing Award. Tomecek also works as a consultant and writer for The National Geographic Society and Scholastic, Inc.